TWENTIETH CENTURY VIEWS

The aim of this series is to present the best
in contemporary critical opinion on major
authors, providing a twentieth century perspective on their changing status in an era
of profound revaluation.

Maynard Mack, *Series Editor*
Yale University

GEORGE ELIOT

A COLLECTION OF CRITICAL ESSAYS

Edited by
George R. Creeger

Prentice-Hall, Inc. *Englewood Cliffs, N. J.*

A SPECTRUM BOOK

Current printing (last number):
10 9 8 7 6

Prentice-Hall International, Inc. *(London)*
Prentice-Hall of Australia, Pty. Ltd. *(Sydney)*
Prentice-Hall of Canada, Ltd. *(Toronto)*
Prentice-Hall of India Private Ltd. *(New Delhi)*
Prentice-Hall of Japan, Inc. *(Tokyo)*

Contents

Prefatory Note

The bulk of George Eliot criticism is very large, as even the selected bibliography at the end of this volume suggests. The quality is also generally high, so that problems of making a representative and, at the same time, relatively small selection were difficult. For each of the articles chosen there were always at least another two or three possibilities. The reader will find such alternates included in the bibliography.

With two exceptions, this anthology reprints material that has not been reprinted earlier; and with one exception it draws upon recent work. The single exception (James's "*Daniel Deronda:* A Conversation") needs a word of explanation, perhaps of defense: the most straightforward reason for its presence is that it finally proved impossible to exclude. It has, of course, been reprinted; its view of *Daniel Deronda* is, if stimulating, a limited one; and at times it is offensive to modern sensibilities. Nevertheless, it remains one of those articles on George Eliot that every student should know, in part because of its intrinsic vitality but also because it marks the beginning of a tradition in George Eliot criticism that has persisted to our own time.

The Introduction that follows possesses a double function. Based to some extent upon the articles themselves, it seeks to set forth in anticipatory fashion some of the important ideas presented more fully in the articles. At the same time it is intended as a brief account of George Eliot's characteristic qualities of mind, her major themes, and her theory and practice of fiction. Such a *multum in parvo* can never be satisfactory, but it may serve as a kind of initial (or renewing) stimulus for coming to grips with George Eliot's work.

In preparing this anthology the editor turned for advice—all of it good though not all of it taken—to colleagues engaged in George Eliot studies. I should like especially to thank Professor Gordon S. Haight, in whose debt stand all of us interested in George Eliot and her work; and Professors Richard Lyons, Joseph Reed, Jr., and James Wheatley. For assistance in tracking down articles I am grateful to Messrs. Abdulla ab-Dabbagh, John Crigler, and Helmut Volger. For patience and encouragement, as well as advice, I should like to thank the General Editor of this series, Professor Maynard Mack.

Introduction

by George R. Creeger

George Eliot has rarely lacked either grateful readers or perceptive critics, although their number has fluctuated. In her own time they were legion: Mrs. Carlyle, who had been beguiled of a night's severe pain by *Scenes of Clerical Life*, declared that *Adam Bede* "was as good as *going into the country for one's health*." Dickens wrote that the same book had "taken its place among the actual experiences and endurances of . . . [his] life." Frederic Harrison wondered if it were right, in the case of *Felix Holt*, to give a work of fiction "the subtle finish of a poem." [1] And Henry James, declaring jocosely to his father that he had fallen in love "with this great horse-faced blue-stocking," [2] exercised his devotion by becoming one of her most astute critics. The appreciation and discrimination displayed by such contemporaries were exhibited less frequently by their successors, although no decade, with only an occasional exception, failed of at least one perceptive critic; and the years following the second world war have seen a dramatic rise in their number. Today her reputation stands as high as it did a hundred years ago.

Nevertheless, in over a century of criticism[3] one rarely encounters unqualified praise. Instead there is a persistent and petulant desire to have George Eliot different from what she was. Her publisher, John Blackwood, while perfectly willing to second Lewes's cry "What a stupendous genius it is!" [4] was nevertheless perturbed by

1. *The George Eliot Letters*, ed. Gordon S. Haight (New Haven: Yale University Press, 1954–55), III, 17; III, 114; IV, 284–85.
2. Quoted by Gordon S. Haight, *George Eliot: A Biography* (Oxford: At the Clarendon Press, 1968), p. 417.
3. A useful survey is *A Century of George Eliot Criticism*, ed. Gordon S. Haight (Boston: Houghton Mifflin Company, 1965).
4. Haight, *Letters*, VI, 196.

the moral daring of his author. James, of all people, who saw *Middlemarch* as setting "a limit . . . to the development of the old-fashioned English novel," lamented "the loss of simplicity" and deplored the obscurity of "a dozen passages" in the book.[5] Of the same work Virginia Woolf offered the high but qualified praise that it was, "with all its imperfections . . . one of the few English novels written for grown-up people." [6] And there was a time when Dr. Leavis was willing to do away completely with the Jewish part of *Daniel Deronda,* giving to the remainder the title of *Gwendolen Harleth.*

Such attitudes are naturally heterogeneous, springing from no single impulse and difficult, therefore, to bring under any single explanation. Yet perhaps they find a common tone in such a hypothetical lament as the following: "If only George Eliot had been born a Flaubert, or a Tolstoy, or a Proust!" If, in fact, she had been a great Continental novelist rather than what she was: a great but thoroughly English one. For despite her cosmopolitan experience and her involvement with the intellectual life of the Continent (particularly of Germany) she remained invincibly English. The evidence is everywhere: in her letters, in her essays and reviews, and preeminently in her novels. This Englishness, which James thought likely to be particularly clear to American readers, may not altogether account for her habits of mind, or for the themes and techniques of her fiction, but it is a convenient point of departure.

For example, it helps to define what remains (after the comprehensive power of her intellect and its singular fusion with deep feeling) a principal characteristic of George Eliot's mind—her intense conservatism. The word suggests a political orientation and can be understood in that sense, but it includes a great deal more: the value, amounting almost to piety, she gave to the past; the stress she placed upon duty; the insistence that the passions stood in need of a controlling rationality; the acceptance of change and a belief in progress qualified by a fear that any abrupt wrenching would prove harmful to the structure of society; and the yearning, while in London and at the very heart of the world's greatest

---

5. In his review of *Middlemarch* (see Haight, *A Century of George Eliot Criticism,* pp. 86–87).

6. Quoted in Haight, *A Century of George Eliot Criticism,* p. 187.

mercantile and industrial power, for a preindustrial age she had known as a child among the green fields and hedgerows of rural England.

Yet this conservatism was balanced, as Cross noted in his biography (1885), by strong liberal-reforming tendencies—or if not precisely balanced, then set off in a state of tension. Tension, in turn, is a second important aspect of her mind. Psychologically regarded, it was the conflict between a powerfully sensuous nature and an equally strong impulse toward asceticism and renunciation. This interior tension naturally manifested itself, however disguised, in her public life: while she was willing to flout social taboos in order to enter a permanent union with George Henry Lewes, the action was performed and sustained at great psychic cost. For proof there is the record of her classically psychosomatic headaches and "renal disorders." This same tension made it difficult for her to live at ease in London, though for many years duty and necessity conspired to keep her there. Yet relief from bodily suffering together with a renewed sense of freedom and vitality often lay no farther away than Kent or Sussex, or if not in the English countryside, then in the relaxed and undemanding moral atmosphere of Italy or Germany.

The tension of George Eliot's mind need not, however, be understood quite so narrowly: in broader terms it can be seen as representing an intellectual malaise from which scarcely a great mind of the century was free—whether that of Mill, Carlyle, Marx, Melville, or Dostoevsky. Such minds, all one way or another legatees of European romanticism, had explored too deeply the hidden landscapes of the psyche, were too aware of suffering and injustice despite progress, and too convinced of the probable certainty of God's death to accept with complacency the rational and optimistic shibboleths of the age. Yet this fact of unease, though it could prove debilitating (never more clearly than in the case of Mill) was also a potent source of energy; it served well as subject matter for much discursive and narrative writing; and it proved, I would suggest, a basis for the century's most characteristic pattern of thought— that of Hegelian dialectic, with its thesis and antithesis resolving themselves, but not coming to final rest, in synthesis.

A third aspect of George Eliot's mind needs to be mentioned, and

that is its pronounced moral cast. At its lowest level her sense of
morality partook merely of English bourgeois prudery: Byron she
declared "the most *vulgar-minded* genius that ever produced a great
effect in literature." [7] Of Heine, whose greatness she helped to
establish in the minds of the English, she nevertheless thought that
a "friendly penknife" might be necessary to remove the more scrof-
ulous passages from a volume of his to make it fit for the eyes of
young readers.[8] And as for the French! Though she expressed sorrow for the suffering of that unhappy nation during the Franco-
Prussian war (itself brought about by "an iniquitous Government"),
she went resolutely on to assert that there was "in a great proportion
of the French people . . . a wicked glorification of selfish pride,
which like all other conceit is a sort of stupidity, excluding any true
conception of what lies outside their own vain wishes." [9]

Such a judgment is a caricature; but take away the object judged
("the French people"), regard simply the basis of judgment, and one
sees that the smugness and parochialism are accidental. What George
Eliot attacks is the dominance of self to the exclusion of all that lies
outside it. As a concept of immorality, this is very old; it is distinc-
tively Christian in its formulation; and it constitutes the ground of
George Eliot's ethic. Repeatedly she makes the assertion, overtly in
her essays and letters, obliquely in her fiction, that the central evil
is the predilection for self over others. When she wanted to render
her notion of Hell concrete, she summoned the image of people
crowding a gambling table at a German spa. But such a scene
dramatized evil for her not because of the gambling itself but because of the monomaniacal self-absorption of those involved.[10]

Her passionate conviction that man's greatest immorality lay in
modes of narcissism found a counterposition in the belief that
Heaven, to continue the metaphor, could exist in Hell's despite:
it is the condition that she called variously "fellow-feeling," and
"sympathy." No matter how powerful the mind, unless there is a
concomitant capacity for compassion, there can be no escape from
the prison of the self. Some rare and lucky human beings are born

---

7. Haight, *Letters*, V, 57.

8. "German Wit: Heinrich Heine," in *Essays of George Eliot,* ed. Thomas
Pinney (London: Routledge and Kegan Paul, 1963), p. 224.

9. Haight, *Letters*, V, 113.

10. See Haight, *Letters*, V, 312 and Bk. I, Ch. 1 of *Daniel Deronda.*

free; most men have to achieve freedom, and the process is difficult, as the testimony of George Eliot's fiction makes clear. When she voiced fear in a letter that her father's death would mean the disappearance of "part of [her] moral nature," she added: "I had a horrid vision of myself . . . becoming earthly sensual and devilish for want of that purifying restraining influence." [11] The language is erotic, but it was not so much her sexuality that produced anxiety as the possibility that without the principle of restraint embodied by her father, that sexuality would lead her to selfishness. It was this condition that would be "devilish."

All three of these characteristics of her mind—its conservatism, tension, and morality—naturally find expression in her fiction, the principal themes of which I should like to consider next. Any attempt at a brief statement of them will necessarily seem sketchy and abstract; however, for the essential stability of what George Eliot called "the point of view from which I regard . . . life" we have her own word: "there has been," she declared, "no change . . . since I wrote my first fiction . . . Any apparent change of spirit must be due to something of which I am unconscious. The principles which are at the root of my effort to paint Dinah Morris [*Adam Bede*] are equally at the root of my effort to paint Mordecai" [*Daniel Deronda*].[12] On the basis of such an assertion one is justified in setting up a paradigmatic narrative situation for her fiction. By means of this paradigm one can arrive, in turn, at a reasonably clear, if foreshortened, view of her major themes.

Characteristically, the following kind of situation is likely to obtain in a George Eliot novel: despite the presence of a fully conceived and often minutely reproduced society, the principal emphasis falls upon the problems of an individual. This individual, usually young and inexperienced, is presented as intellectually capable and emotionally intense but morally obtuse. The cause of the obtuseness is almost invariably a form of pride—the blindness of egoism. This bright, intense, but egoistic self lives unfulfilled; in its obtuseness it believes that fulfillment will be possible if its private desires are gratified. To that end it attaches itself to another individual, most often in a relationship that the self regards as love.

11. Haight, *Letters*, I, 284.
12. Haight, *Letters*, VI, 318.

Unwilling in this relationship, however, to give up any of the imperative demands of self, and at the same time expecting everything from the other, the egoistic self sets in motion a series of events that lead toward catastrophe.

The self, in its attempt to achieve fulfillment through the gratification of private desires, causes the destruction or wounding of the other self (or selves) upon which it has been battening. In so doing, it is brought to a dead standstill and forced to survey both the wreckage it has caused and the barrenness in which it lives. Sometimes the wreckage involves a literal death; and where it does not, death is nevertheless metaphorically present in the form of privation and suffering—the necessary preconditions, in George Eliot's scheme of things, for any radical reorientation of personality.

At this nadir, and precisely because of the intensity of its suffering, the self is permitted a new vision of the world: it comes to recognize the relative meanness of its private desires; it is forced to grant the autonomy of other selves; it perceives that in the larger world outside itself there is a moral order (a universal law or nemesis) which, though there may well be no God, operates just as effectively as if there were; and it admits the necessity of renouncing the imperious demands of the self and of accepting the fact of limits. Both this renunciation and acceptance imply a conception of duty under whose yoke the self is now willing to live. If it is very lucky, it need not live alone, for although eros has been transmuted in part to sympathy, there has been no loss of passion; and the selfless love of another, a genuine "thou," enables the hitherto selfish ego to extend its sympathy from individual human beings to humanity at large. In so doing the self achieves full consciousness and maturity. Not all of George Eliot's egoists achieve this quality of consciousness, but the motion toward it constitutes the basic pattern of her narratives.

From this pattern George Eliot's themes stand out in sharp relief. At the center is egoism which, among man's vices, is the cardinal one, a precise equivalent of pride. This human failing, with its attendant selfishness and blindness, is the source, in turn, of most of the woes that afflict man. Redemption from egoism is possible, but the process requires drastic measures, so nearly impervious to outside claims is the egoistic self. Only suffering has sufficient power to break through the carapace within which the self lives. The necessity of suffering becomes, then, a second major theme. A third and fourth have to do with what the self comes to accept as a result of suffering—namely, the presence of Law at the heart of the universe; and the "peremptory and absolute" nature of Duty (as George Eliot once pronounced it) with its stress upon acceptance, endurance, and renunciation. Finally there is the theme of redemption and regeneration, presented in her fiction as an escape from egoism and as the discovery of temperate happiness by sensing one's kinship with mankind.

The ways in which these themes—thus bluntly stated—achieve complexity and vitality in George Eliot's novels the student will discover for himself. It may be well, however, to offer a few preliminary suggestions about the theory and practice of her fiction.

George Eliot held a number of views about novel-writing that amounted almost to axioms and that were characteristic of most of her fiction from *Scenes of Clerical Life* to *Daniel Deronda*. The first of these was realism, by which she meant primarily a fidelity to the world in which we live. Early in her career George Eliot meant a *minute* fidelity to that world;[13] later she came to modify her position somewhat and to permit the imagination more play. Still, she never wholly abandoned her belief that art is to give us life as it really is. "The sculptor," she once wrote in praise of Houdon's bust of Gluck, "has given every scar made by the small-pox; he has left the nose as pug and insignificant, and the mouth as common, as Nature made them; but then he has done what, doubtless, Nature also did." [14]

A second tenet of her theory of fiction is that of unity. Even before she began to write novels, she had developed a clear idea of what unity in a work of art is. "An opera," she wrote in 1855, "must be no mosaic of melodies stuck together with no other method than is supplied by accidental contrast . . . but an organic whole, which grows up like a palm, its earliest portion containing the germ and prevision of all the rest." [15] Again, this early notion

13. See for example her letter to Chapman of 12 [July] 1857 (Haight, *Letters,* II, 362) and Ch. 17 of *Adam Bede.*
14. Pinney, *Essays,* p. 88.
15. Pinney, *Essays,* p. 102.

of unity underwent development, so that later in her life it came to mean "the relationship of multiplex interdependent parts to a whole which is itself in the most varied & therefore the fullest relation to other wholes." [16] But even for this more complex idea of unity an organic metaphor (this time the human body) remained an appropriate means of making the abstraction concrete.

A third tenet of her theory is that fiction serves the ends of teaching. She herself particularly disliked didactic novels, yet at no point in her career did she ever completely abandon the idea that novels serve to instruct their readers. The basis of this idea lay in her belief that art "is the nearest thing to life; it is a mode of amplifying experience and extending our contact with our fellowmen beyond the bounds of our personal lot." [17] Inevitably then any "man or woman who publishes writings . . . assumes the office of teacher or influencer of the public mind." [18] The ultimate aim of art is to reshape human consciousness and with it the structure of society, although the process is necessarily a slow one since, as she wrote toward the end of her life, man's nature "can only be wrought on by little and little." [19]

Theory converts to practice, or, alternatively, theory derives from practice; in either case practice must not be ignored. Yet to discuss all the major aspects of George Eliot's novelistic technique—structure, plotting, narrative method, tone, imagery, symbolism, characterization—is clearly out of the question here. However, it is possible to choose a single problem and to assign it representative power—not that all other problems are wholly subsumed under this particular one, but it does have the merit of long life; furthermore, it has almost invariably elicited that petulant tone of which I spoke at the beginning; and it points to characteristics of George Eliot's technique that must be faced if the reader is to approach her novels with pleasure and understanding.

"One thing I do not like," a contemporary wrote, "is the habit of putting her characters at a distance as if to look at them and then making remarks on them." [20] The basic charge made here (and it

16. Pinney, *Essays*, p. 433.
17. Pinney, *Essays*, p. 271.
18. Pinney, *Essays*, p. 440.
19. Haight, *Letters*, VII, 346.
20. Haight, *Letters*, V, 254.

has been reiterated dozens of times) is that George Eliot speaks too often in her own person, steps in too frequently to maneuver her characters, is in short altogether too meddlesome. She should, the argument runs, stay out of the picture entirely, leaving her characters alone and us free to judge them independently. At this juncture the most direct and naive question is perhaps the most appropriate: Why? A standard answer is that Henry James said so. Granted, the reason is formidable, but despite its authority, it does not constitute an invariable rule of fiction. There are, in fact, no general rules of fiction, whatever specific ones exist for the perfect Jamesian novel: George Eliot, like Sterne before and Joyce after her, was a free agent; what rules existed she created as she wrote.

There are more subtle reasons, however, for not only defending George Eliot's right to become a voice in her fiction but asserting that her fiction benefits as a result. For one thing, the sheer bulk of her novels permits a digressive leisureliness—perhaps even demands it. Our sense of pace is usually gratified not outraged by the digressions, asides, or the analyses of character. Furthermore, the quality of her mind is so high, her insights so keen, that we find what she writes discursively of immediate interest. (There is a sense in which she is not only more intelligent than any of her characters, she is also more interesting.) In addition, her becoming a voice in the novel permits a dialectic between the "legitimate" characters and an observing critical intelligence, and also between action rendered dramatically and action understood. The reader is thereby permitted both to see and to understand. One problem has been that George Eliot's analyses have been regarded as prescriptive—as a demand that characters and actions be understood only in the terms of the analysis given. Rightly perceived, however, the discursive passages are no more prescriptive than the dramatic ones: both are, in fact, invitations—on the one hand to observation of action, on the other to analysis. Our freedom as readers to make up our own minds is not impaired.

Finally, one might argue that there is a fitness about the technique, given the age in which the novels were written and the temperament of their author. To require of nineteenth-century intelligences that they remove themselves completely from the arena of action is a nearly unthinkable demand: it was an age of involvement, whether with a world of objective or of imagined fact. George Eliot's contemporaries knew this and confirmed it by creating of her a sibylline figure. This figure has often been rejected; but she has great powers of survival, and it may be that our own decade, less self-conscious about wisdom than others have been, will welcome the return of the Wise Woman and read her words attentively.

George Eliot's Religion of Humanity

by Bernard J. Paris

The real crisis in George Eliot's history came not when she broke with Christianity, but when she broke with pantheism, for only then did she have to ask herself if life has any meaning without God. After her rejection of Christianity in the early 1840's, Eliot still lived in a universe which was divinely sustained and directed; and although she no longer believed in personal immortality, she still felt that man's spiritual nature linked him to God. From Hennell, Spinoza, Wordsworth, Carlyle, and Bray, she derived a pantheism in which God is immanent in the laws of nature and the mind of man. The universe is benevolently disposed towards man and is responsive to the needs of the human heart. The "Soul of the World," wrote Hennell, "is a principle bearing close relationship to man's heart, and beaming forth through all material things to the intellectual eye." [1] The purpose of life, the highest good, is to know and love God, to put oneself in harmony with His will. By endowing all existence with a divine presence and purpose, pantheism satisfied George Eliot's need for a sense of religious orientation in the cosmos.

But the positivistic teachings of Comte, Mill, Spencer, Lewes, and Feuerbach, which formed the foundation of Eliot's thought from the early 1850's on, placed man in an indifferent universe which provided neither a response to his consciousness nor a sanction for his values. The positivistic cosmology led Eliot to see life as essentially tragic, the tragedy lying in the disparity between the

"George Eliot's Religion of Humanity" by Bernard J. Paris. From *English Literary History*, XXIX (December, 1962), 418–43. Copyright © 1962 by The Johns Hopkins Press. Reprinted by permission of The Johns Hopkins Press.

1. Charles Christian Hennell, *Christian Theism* (London, 1939), p. 53.

inward and the outward, between the passionate impulses and needs of man and the dispassionate order of things which more often than not frustrates human will and desire. Scientific knowledge offered the prospect of meliorating power over the course of things, but man would always need to be reconciled to the pain which is an inevitable consequence of his unequal struggle with the forces outside himself. The great question for Eliot, as well as for many of her contemporaries and ours, was, how can man lead a meaningful, morally satisfying life in an absurd universe?

What Eliot needed, of course, was a new religion, a religion which would mediate between man and the alien cosmos, as the old religions had done, but which would do so without escaping into illusion, without denying that the cosmos is, indeed, alien. With the old consolations gone, what was to sustain man through a painful existence (his only one) in a blind, indifferent universe? Eliot did not seek new consolations so much as a means of reconciling man to the realities of his lot. She wrote to Sara Hennell: "The test of a higher religion might be, that it should enable the believer to do without the consolations which his egoism would demand." [2] Eliot sympathized with those who needed the support of conventional religion, for she saw that we all need a sense of belonging, a way of sustaining loneliness and frustration, a means of somehow understanding and controlling the indifferent, mysterious otherness outside of ourselves. Eliot felt that the power and value of traditional religion lay in its ability to satisfy these needs, and she had no wish to disturb those whose needs were so strong that they were unable to face reality or to do with less than the absolute satisfactions of orthodox belief. But she felt that it was possible to satisfy man's need for a sense of moral relation to the world, though not, certainly, all of his egoistic cravings, without the illusion of God. Indeed, she had the optimistic belief, so characteristic of her time, that facing the painful truth would eventually lead man to a higher life and a nobler religion than any he had known. "I have faith," she wrote to Mme. Bodichon, "in the working-out of higher

2. *The George Eliot Letters,* ed. Gordon S. Haight (New Haven, 1954–55), v, 69. Hereafter in citing this edition I shall simply give the volume and page numbers parenthetically in the text.

possibilities than the Catholic or any other church has presented, and those who have strength to wait and endure, are bound to accept no formula which their whole souls—their intellect as well as their emotions—do not embrace with entire reverence. The highest 'calling and election' is to *do without opium* and live through all our pain with conscious, clear-eyed endurance" (III, 366).

The religion of the future, Eliot felt, would be a religion not of God, but of man, a religion of humanity. Feuerbach taught, in fact, that the religions of the past have been truly religions of humanity, but unconsciously so; the religion of the future will consciously worship man. The central preoccupation of George Eliot's life was with religion, and in her novels, which she thought of as "experiments in life," she was searching for a view of life that would give modern man a sense of purpose, dignity, and ethical direction. She wrote to Clifford Allbutt: "The inspiring principle which alone gives me courage to write is, that of so presenting our human life as to help my readers in getting a clearer conception and a more active admiration of those vital elements which bind man together and give a higher worthiness to their existence" (IV, 472). That the "vital elements" of which Eliot here speaks are natural rather than supernatural, human rather than divine, is made perfectly clear by a letter to Mrs. Ponsonby in which Eliot asserts that her novels have "for their main bearing" the conclusion that "the fellowship between man and man which has been the principle of development, social and moral, is not dependent on conceptions of what is not man; and that the idea of God, so far as it has been a high spiritual influence, is the ideal of a goodness entirely human (i.e., an exaltation of the human)" (VI, 98). I am not, of course, concerned to show that George Eliot did not believe in God—that is well known—but to see what she put in place of God, how she went about constructing her religion of humanity.[3]

3. In the account of Eliot's philosophy which follows I have made no special effort either to demonstrate that Eliot actually believed what I say she did or to show how her beliefs are dramatized in her novels—to do either would require a much longer essay. I have tried, rather, to present a systematic and condensed account of Eliot's quest for values.

I

The order of things is unconscious, unresponsive to man, un-related to human desires and values; but there is, in Eliot's view, another order, a human, moral order, which *is* responsive to con-sciousness and which *is* a source and sanction of moral values. The moral order is manifested in love and fellow-feeling between indi-viduals, in the products and traditions of human culture, in the laws and institutions of society, in the creeds, symbols, and cere-monies of religion; in general, in any human institution or activity which by interposing itself between the individual and the alien cosmos lessens the disparity between the inward and the outward and humanizes the world. The moral order is not independent of the cosmic or non-moral order, but exists within it and is in some respects a product of it. Darwin, Spencer, Lewes, and Huxley ex-plained that the cosmic process, which has no relation to moral ends, produced human society, or what Huxley called the ethical process, by virtue of the survival value of social union. Since those societies whose members were most devoted to the common welfare were naturally selected, the cosmic process, whose principle is ag-gressiveness and competition, gave rise to the ethical process, the moral order, whose principle is cooperation.

The moral order is an evolved order, but its evolution differs from that found in the non-moral order in that it is produced and directed in some degree by human feeling and conscious purpose, casual agencies which are entirely absent in non-moral evolution. Thus moral evolution is often in conflict with the tendencies of non-moral evolution; the function of the moral order, in fact, is to ameliorate the suffering caused by the non-moral conditions of life. Huxley argued that "in place of ruthless self-assertion" the ethical process "demands self-restraint, in place of thrusting aside, or tread-ing down all competitors, it requires that the individual shall not merely respect but shall help his fellows; its influence is directed, not so much to the survival of the fittest, as to the fitting of as many as possible to survive." [4] In a letter to John Morley in which she

4. *Evolution and Ethics and Other Essays* (London, 1894), p. 82. Huxley's essays on "Evolution and Ethics" did not, of course, influence Eliot, but their

attempted to clarify her views on the proper position of women in society Eliot attacked "the 'intention of Nature' argument," which, she said, is "a pitiable fallacy." Not nature, not biological evolution which is indifferent to human suffering, but human feeling is the proper source of social goals. "As a fact of mere zoological evolution," Eliot argued, woman has "the worse share in existence. But for that very reason I would the more contend that in the moral evolution we have 'an art which does mend nature.' It is the function of love in the largest sense, to mitigate the harshness of all fatalities." The mission of the human order is to "lighten the pressure of hard non-moral outward conditions" (IV, 364–65).

George Eliot spoke of G. H. Lewes' concept of the Social Factor in Psychology as "the supremely interesting element in the thinking of our time" (VII, 161). According to Lewes, human psychic phenomena cannot be fully explained unless they are regarded as the products of our organic inheritance from the past—of the "psychological evolution of sociological material"—and of our interaction with the super-organically evolved social medium.[5] Man is a product of both the animal kingdom and the social organism—"the soul of man has thus a double root, a double history." [6] Man's egoistic impulses, his concern for himself at the expense of others, are manifestations of his animal nature; but his moral life, his desire for the welfare of others, is largely the consequence of his relation to society. Civilization, not primitive nature, is the source of our highest life and greatest good.

Although the higher animals have structures much like our own, they are separated from us by an impassable barrier due to the fact that their experiences have never become generalized in an impersonal social organism which at once shapes and is shaped by all subsequent experience. Human society owes its existence to the evolution in man of consciousness, the faculty which enables man to separate the self from the not-self and objects from feelings. Consciousness is the primary source of the moral order; it produces

---

terminology is convenient and most of the ideas they express were current in the 1860's and 1870's.

5. *Problems of Life and Mind: First Series. The Foundations of a Creed* (London, 1874–75), I, 134.

6. *Ibid.*, p. 125.

that awareness of species, of others as distinct from yet like ourselves, which is the basis of all ethical action, of the sense of solidarity with our kind which leads us to sacrifice our own immediate gratification for the good of others. "The law of animal action," writes Lewes, "is Individualism; its motto is 'Each for himself against all.' The ideal of human action is Altruism; its motto is 'Each *with* others, all for each.' " [7]

In society, with its traditions, creeds, institutions, laws, and ceremonials, and in the sentiments which their social heritage and identification inspire in the breasts of individuals, the moral order has a potent existence. In his relations to society, hereditary and assumed, are defined the individual's duties and his identity. Those who cut themselves off from their society find, like Don Silva in *The Spanish Gypsy,* that "on solitary souls, the universe / Looks down inhospitable; the human heart / Finds nowhere shelter but in human kind." [8] The moral lives of George Eliot's characters—their sense of duty and rectitude, of personal significance and spiritual satisfaction—are very largely determined by the extent to which the social experience of the race and the will of society have shaped their attitudes, and by the degree to which they feel themselves to be part of a corporate existence which is greater than themselves. Tradition, Eliot felt, is "the basis of our best life"; moral life is based on sentiment, and "our sentiments may be called organized traditions" (*Essays,* p. 181). Sentiment saves existence from absurdity, for it hallows and sanctifies that which reason finds meaningless or relative. Sentiment moves us to acts of goodness, of unselfishness, of reverence, for which reason provides no motivation or rationale. In morality reason is the servant of desire; socially inspired sentiments are far more trustworthy as guides and effective as sources of ethical action. One of the most valuable social feelings, for Eliot, is the sense of identification with a racial, political, social, or religious group, or with an historical tradition—the feeling of being part of a worthy corporate body. "Our dignity and rectitude," Eliot wrote, "are proportioned to our sense of relationship with

7. *The Study of Psychology* (Boston, 1879), p. 137.
8. *The Spanish Gypsy,* p. 312. All quotations from Eliot's novels, poems, and collected essays are from the Cabinet Edition of *The Works of George Eliot* (Edinburgh and London, 1878-80).

something great, admirable, pregnant with high possibilities, worthy of sacrifice, a continual inspiration to self-repression and discipline by the presentation of aims larger and more attractive than the securing of personal ease or prosperity" (*Impressions of Theophrastus Such,* pp. 266–67).

Morality springs not only from tradition and its inward reflexes in conscience and sentiment, but also from "the sympathetic impulses that need no law" (*Romola,* Ch. IX). Indeed, the noblest and most enduring parts of tradition are formulations of sympathetic experience, and sympathy is important in rendering the individual sensitive to the values of his society. The sympathetic tendencies may be encouraged by tradition, but sympathy is antecedent to tradition and potentially superior to it. The individual who has a strongly sympathetic nature combined with profound personal experience and the ability to imagine the inner states of others has a moral life that is independent of tradition; he has a more highly developed conscience and a truer sense of good and evil than tradition, in its present state of development, could supply. The sympathetic tendencies can lead a person to rebel against the harsh usages of tradition, even when such rebellion involves great personal risk.

The positivist psychology taught that man is innately social and sympathetic. These qualities were initially products of the cosmic process; they arose through random variation and were naturally selected because of their survival value. They have been considerably strengthened by habit and by the encouraging influence of the social medium; but their development has been slow because moral evolution has been impeded by lack of high intelligence in the great mass of men and by competition between and within societies, which prevents the giving of sympathy to members of antagonistic groups (though it knits men together within the group). A sympathetic feeling is one which is excited by the signs of feeling in another person; intelligence, mental vision, is needed to read the signs. Sympathy and vision are both dependent upon experience. Unless we have had an experience much like that which another person is undergoing, we cannot perceive and share the states of feeling signified by his behavior. Thus Eliot felt that suffering humanizes. Our own suffering, if it does not simply embitter, leads us to be sympathetic with the sufferings of others, and our sympathy leads us to behave so that others will not suffer as we have.

Eliot opposed those who felt that the sole basis of morality is man's selfish desire for reward and fear of punishment. Edward Young, whose religion, she contended, was nothing but "egoism turned heavenward," had made hope of reward and fear of future punishment man's sole inducement to ethical behavior: "If it were not for the prospect of immortality, he considers, it would be wise and agreeable to be indecent . . . ; and, heaven apart, it would be extremely irrational in any man not to be a knave" (*Essays*, p. 45). Eliot, in the person of a hypothetical unbeliever, attributed Young's position to his "utter want of moral emotion":

> I am just and honest, not because I expect to live in another world, but, because, having felt the pain of injustice and dishonesty towards myself, I have a fellow-feeling with other men, who would suffer the same pain if I were unjust or dishonest towards them. . . . The fact is, I do *not* love myself alone, whatever logical necessity there may be for that conclusion in your mind. . . . It is a pang to me to witness the suffering of a fellow-being, and I feel his suffering the more acutely because he is *mortal*—because his life is so short, and I would have it, if possible, filled with happiness and not misery. Through my union and fellowship with the men and women I *have* seen, I feel a like, though fainter, sympathy with those I have *not seen*; and I am able so to live in imagination with the generations to come, that their good is not alien to me, and is a stimulus to me to labour for ends which may not benefit myself, but will benefit them (pp. 52–53).

Our own experience, when combined with vision and sympathy, unites us with others, reducing the disparity between the inward and outward for ourselves, and prompting us to function as mediator for others.

W. H. Mallock contended that apart from the revealed dogmas of Christianity "there is nothing in the constitution of things to produce, to favour, or to demand a course of action called right" (VI, 338). Though George Eliot conceded that Christianity has exerted a potent moral force, she felt that Christianity is important not only because it has profoundly shaped our experience but also because it has *grown out of* human experience. The presence of ethical values and a moral nature in man she attributed not to the agency of God, but to the natural operation of the human ethical process. Instead of morality being initially inspired and sanctioned by religious creeds, religious creeds are originally inspired and sanctioned by the moral emotions and perceptions of mankind. In "A College Breakfast-Party," Guildenstern, who speaks for Eliot, argues that "all sacred rules"

> Can have no form or potency apart
> From the percipient and emotive mind.
> God, duty, love, submission, fellowship
> Must first be framed in man, as music is,
> Before they live outside him as a law.
>   (*The Legend of Jubal and Other Poems,* p. 246)

In her "Notes on 'The Spanish Gypsy'" Eliot observed that "the will of God is the same thing as the will of other men, compelling us to work and avoid what they have seen to be harmful to social existence." [9] The moral order, then, though productive of creeds and dogmas, is not dependent for its origins or continuance upon them. Its chief agent is human feeling—the sympathetic feeling that is the product of experience and vision, and the social sentiment that is produced by the interaction of the individual and the social order.

II

The cosmology, sociology, and psychology of positivism led George Eliot to see reality as composed of an alien cosmos within which there exists a moral order which makes the world habitable for the human spirit and is the source of human values. An equally important contribution to her quest for a religion of humanity was made by the positivist epistemology, which distinguished between two fundamentally different approaches to reality, the objective and the subjective, the empirical and metaphysical.

The positivists branded as metaphysical any philosophy which displayed the following characteristics: (1) a concern with ontology and teleology: (2) a belief either in innate ideas or in laws of thought and categories of perception that do not have their origin in experi-

9. J. W. Cross, *George Eliot's Life as Related in Her Letters and Journals,* Cabinet Ed., III, 39.

ence; (3) a belief in the possibility of an immediate, intuitive knowledge of the existence and nature of a reality which transcends
experience; and (4) a method and test of knowledge which relies
upon introspection, or upon a dialectic which, assuming a built-in
correspondence between the internal and the external, bypasses or
slights sensory experience and works from the inward to the outward. The basic epistemological conceptions of the positivists were:
(1) that experience is the limit of knowledge, and hence that consideration of first and final causes, or of any realm beyond experience, is fruitless and misleading; (2) that we have neither divinely
implanted innate ideas nor imposed categories of perception—the
contents and modes of consciousness are entirely the product of
evolution and experience; (3) that all knowledge of the external
world is relative—i.e., things cannot be known as they are in themselves, but only as they appear to human consciousness; and (4)
that no conception of external reality can be accepted as true without verification, that experience or consonance with experience and
not logical consistency or belief is the test of truth, and that the
objective method—which bends the mind to the outward shows
of things instead of ordering external existence according to the
preconceptions or wishes of the mind—is the only path to truth.

As the positivists see it, the essential characteristic of the subjective or metaphysical method is that it confuses the objective with
the subjective. It converts the internal into the exernal, thereby
making the subjective and objective orders identical. There is no
clear distinction between self and non-self; the world is an extension
of the ego. Abstractions, mental constructs, are reified, are given
an autonomous external existence. The desires of the heart, the
preconceptions of the intellect, and the qualities of human nature
are projected into outer phenomena and are then assumed to have
an objective existence. For the positivists the external world exists
and has an autonomous order which does not necessarily correspond
to the order of thought; truth is pursued by submitting the mind
to the world so that the order of ideas becomes a reflection of the
order of phenomena. The metaphysician, on the other hand, does
not test his speculations by confrontation with external reality; he
pursues knowledge of the external order by introspection, or by

deduction from premises which introspection yields. For him all clear and distinct ideas are true.

The most extreme form of the subjective (or egotistical) approach to external reality is in religion. "The religious mind," writes Feuerbach, "does not distinguish between subjective and objective, —it has no doubts; it has the faculty, not of discerning other things than itself, but of seeing its own conceptions out of itself as distinct beings." [10] The real external order is supplanted by an illusory external order which is simply the subjectivity of the individual made into an object. According to Feuerbach, almost all of religion's conceptions of God and the world are in reality unconscious objectifications of man's own nature, needs, and desires. The religious doctrines of creation out of nothing, providence, prayer, and faith, for example, are all objectifications of man's desire for the obliteration of physical nature and the supremacy of his own subjective personality. By the doctrine of creation out of nothing man resolves the conflict between the resistant otherness of the world and his subjective desires; he removes from his consciousness the awareness of that external order, characterized by ineluctable, impersonal causal sequences, which stands between himself and the absolute. For, Feuerbach argues, "the 'nothing' out of which the world was produced, is a still inherent nothingness. When thou sayest the world was made out of nothing, thou conceivest the world itself as nothing" (p. 109). Consciousness is eternal and supreme, the only thing that really exists. In a world governed by a supernatural Providence, material circumstances are entirely subservient to the will of God, which is, of course, really man's own will projected into objectivity.

"The essence of faith," says Feuerbach," is the idea that that which man wishes actually is" (p. 128). Hope, in the theological sense, is belief in the fulfillment of those wishes which are not yet realized. The object of faith and hope is miracle, for faith and hope are "nothing else than confidence in the reality of the subjective in opposition to the limitations or laws of Nature and reason" (p.

10. *The Essence of Christianity,* 2nd ed., trans. George Eliot (Harper Torchbook, New York, 1957), pp. 204–205. Hereafter referred to as *Essence.* Eliot's translation was first published in London, 1854.

126). Prayer expresses not the dependence of man on external things, but the supremacy of human needs and wishes over all else: "prayer is the unconditional confidence of human feeling in the absolute identity of the subjective and objective, the certainty that the power of the heart is greater than the power of Nature, that the heart's need is absolute necessity, the fate of the world" (p. 123).

Although George Eliot rejected completely Christianity's claim to have the truth about nature and God, she remained always intensely interested in Christianity. The Higher Criticism of Spinoza, Hennell, and Strauss,[11] by showing that Christian records, beliefs, and institutions are human in origin, converted Christianity, for Eliot, into a source of profound truth about the nature of man. To Mme. Bodichon Eliot wrote: "I care only to know, if possible, the lasting meaning that lies in all religious doctrine from the beginning till now" (IV, 65). She cared "for that which is essentially human in all forms of belief," and desired "to exhibit it under all forms with loving truthfulness" (III, 111). Indeed, anyone who reads Eliot's novels with a knowledge of her intellectual development must ask how this earnest agnostic could treat traditional religion so sympathetically, why she made the religious experience the subject of so much of her fiction, and what moral truth she found religion to embody. Hennell and Strauss had been metaphysical in their analyses of the enduring truths contained in Christianity; and neither, as a consequence, had probed very deeply into the psychological sources of Christian beliefs. It was the philosophy of Feuerbach, in combination with her own earlier experiences as a Christian, which led Eliot to her understanding of the subjective reality which Christianity embodies. "With the ideas of Feuerbach," Eliot wrote, "I everywhere agree" (II, 153).

Feuerbach contended that in its true or anthropological essence Christianity is not a religion of God, but of man, a religion of humanity. His approach to Christianity is empirical; he explicitly rejects idealism and embraces realism: "I do not generate the object

11. I refer to Hennell's *An Inquiry Concerning the Origin of Christianity*, David Friedrich Strauss's *The Life of Jesus, Critically Examined* (which Eliot translated), and Spinoza's *Theological-Political Tractate* (which Eliot began to translate).

from the thought, but the thought from the object" (*Essence,* xxxiv). His aim is "the revelation of religion to itself, the awakening of religion to self-consciousness" (xli); he wants to turn the gaze of religion, theology, and speculative philosophy "from the internal towards the external, *i.e.,* I change the object as it is in the imagina· tion to the object as it is in reality" (xxxix). Objective analysis shows that, insofar as it deals with realities, what religion posits about God is true of and has existence in no other being than man: "Man —this is the mystery of religion—projects his being into objectivity, and then again makes himself an object to this projected image of himself thus converted into a subject; he thinks of himself as an object to himself, but as the object of an object, of another being than himself" (pp. 29–30). God and man (the species) are identical in nature and existence, for the predicates of God are the predicates of humanity. God does exist objectively, from the point of view of the individual, in the species; the species, since its predicates are identical with the divine predicates, is God. Man's sense of God (the species) springs from the nature of his consciousness. Man, unlike the lower animals, is aware of both the self and the non-self; he is therefore aware of his essential nature as it exists in the species. "Man," says Feuerbach, "is himself at once I and thou; he can put himself in the place of another, for this reason, that to him his species, his essential nature, and not merely his individuality, is an object of thought" (p. 2). Man's consciousness of his species results in his religious conceptions of Deity and in his longing to unite his individual nature with the Absolute, which he imagines to be God but which is in reality mankind.

The individual feels his own limitation only because he is conscious of the unlimited; he is conscious of infinity and perfection not in himself but in his species. If he feels the species to be limited, he is making his own limitations the limitations of the species. "The *absolute* to man," Feuerbach proclaims, "is his own nature" (p. 5). It is inevitable that man should regard his essential nature as infinite and perfect; for the nature of the species is the highest nature that he knows, that he can possibly know. The nature of the species is the absolute limit of human consciousness; therefore, to human consciousness the nature of the species is absolute, infinite, perfect. To think of the species as infinite and imperfect, we must regard it from the point of view of a higher nature; but this is impossible, for then we would ourselves have to have this higher nature—the limit of the nature, Feuerbach argues, is the limit of the consciousness belonging to that nature. The predicates which man gives to God must be the predicates of the species. The antithesis between the divine and human natures is illusory; it is but the antithesis between what human nature is capable of and the capabilities of the individual. Since the objects and contents of Christianity are in reality human, Christianity is no absurdity, no record of meaningless phantasies or mistakes of thought, but the repository of real human experiences, the key to man's subjective, moral nature. Feuerbach wants to make Christianity humanly mean-ingful, to resolve metaphysics into psychology and to destroy the unhuman elements in religion—that is, the doctrines of religious objectivism.

As we have seen, Feuerbach regarded many Christian doctrines as the expression of man's egoistic desire for unlimited subjectivity. Christianity is "the dream of waking consciousness" (p. 141); the actions of a providential, miracle-working God reveal "the absolute self-love of man" (p. 127). But Christianity is not only wish-fulfill-ment; it is also self-contemplation—"God is the mirror of man" (p. 63). God has the divine predicates—love, wisdom, justice, etc.— not because he is God, but because the predicates are, in the eyes of man, Godly, worthy of veneration, the highest. The rank of Godhead belongs not to the subject (when God is considered a being apart from the species), but to the predicates. When Chris-tianity says that God is Love, what is really meant is that Love is God. Christianity tells us what qualities of the species man pro-foundly admires; but admiration, worship, have true religious value only when they are bestowed not upon a God imagined to exist apart from the species, but upon the true God of man, Mankind. The secret of Christianity, says Feuerbach, is atheism, the worship of man as God and the denial of any God who is not man. Chris-tianity itself "makes God become man, and then constitutes this God, not distinguished from man, having a human form, human feelings, and human thoughts, the object of its worship and veneration" (xxxvi). The real God of Christianity is Christ, and Christ is "the idea of the species as an individual" (p. 153). The mystery of the Incarnation, says Feuerbach, is the consciousness of the divine love, of God, as human. Since out of love for man God renounced his divinity and became human, "love is a higher power and truth than deity. Love conquers God" (p. 53).

The truth in the doctrine of Christ as savior from sin and suffering is, according to Feuerbach, that love, for man, is a higher power than moral law, that through love man is saved from that soul-destroying sense of worthlessness and alienation from his kind which is the concomitant of a sense of sinfulness. In his consciousness of God as a lawgiver, as a morally perfect being, the individual experiences a painful sense of distance from God, of disparity between his own nature and the divine nature. Man is delivered from "the distressing sense of his own nothingness" by virtue of the fact "that he is conscious of *love* as the highest, the absolute power and truth, that he regards the Divine Being not only as a law, as a moral being, as a being of the understanding; but also as a loving, tender, even subjective human being" (p. 47). The divine love, the suffering, self-sacrificing, forgiving love of Christ, is identical with the highest human love, which Feuerbach suggests, has a saving power similar to that claimed for Christ's love. The statement that God loves man, which is the very central point of religion, means, in actuality, that "the highest is the love of man" (p. 58). The highest, truest teaching of Christianity, then, is that man's love for man is divine, that to love, pity, and suffer for others is to be as God.

Religion, then, for Feuerbach, and for George Eliot, consists pre-eminently in the love, admiration, sympathy and sacrifice of man for man. Human relationships are by their very nature religious in character: "The relations of child and parent," writes Feuerbach, "of husband and wife, of brother and friend—in general, of man to man,—in short, all the moral relations are *per se* religious" (p. 271). Man becomes aware of the species and partakes in its life—lives a truly human and religious life—through his relationship with another human being, with a Thou. To the individual another human being is the representative of the species and his objective conscience. In love the reality of the species becomes a matter of feeling. It is beyond the scope of this essay to demonstrate it, but the fact is that George Eliot conceived of Christianity and of human relationships in a thoroughly Feuerbachian way, and the relations between the characters in her novel are religious in their nature and import. Eliot felt that Tennyson's "In Memoriam" "enshrines the highest tendency of this age" because, whatever was its immediate prompting and "whatever the form under which the author represented his aim to himself, the deepest significance of the poem is the sanctification of human love as a religion." [12]

The great division among George Eliot's characters is between egoists and those who approach reality objectively. The complications of her plots frequently stem from the egoism of central characters; and the development of the action often hinges upon or produces the education of the protagonist from egoism to objectivity, from a morally destructive life of selfishness to the religion of humanity. In Eliot's view we are all born egoists. Both the individual and the race in their childhood regard the world almost entirely from the subjective point of view. Maturation is the process of recognizing the independent existence of outer phenomena (including other people), of yielding up the absolute supremacy of the self.

There are three basic ways, in Eliot's novels, in which self relates to the world. Self may relate to the world egoistically (or subjectively), in which case the distinction between the inward and the outward is obscured; self is seen as the center of the world and the world as an extension of self. Self may be overwhelmed and threatened with annihilation by the hard reality of the world; in this state of disillusionment or disenchantment the world, even the human order, is seen as a totally alien, non-human existence and self as dehumanized, as completely insignificant and spiritually homeless. Or self, retaining its integrity, but giving up its egocentricity, may relate to the world at once meaningfully and objectively, seeing the world as an autonomous existence of which it is a part.

The egoist sees all things in their relation to self rather than in their relations to each other. He tends to assume that the order of things corresponds to the desires of the mind; and instead of cultivating a true vision of casual sequences, he delights in imaginatively shaping the future into accord with present wishes. The egoist has

---

12. "Belles Lettres," *Westminster Review,* LXIV (Oct., 1855), 312.

a vague idea that the ease, luxury, love, and respect that he so earnestly desires must (or should) somehow come to him because he so earnestly desires them and because his own worthiness (beauty, good taste, ability to enjoy, etc.) makes him so deserving of them. The egoist is often a gambler; he may engage in actual games of chance, or he may be a worshipper of Fortune and live in hope that the realization of his desires or escape from punishment for wrongdoing will somehow be granted to him. The egoist frequently has a love of power, a craving for mastery over other people as well as over the course of events. Sometimes he has the illusion that others must want to do what he wants them to do; and sometimes he very deliberately contrives to have them act as he wishes. The feelings of others are given no importance.

Since his desires are not chastened by submission to law and his actions are not governed by a true vision of the relations of things, the egoist is truly at the mercy of circumstances, and his desires are more often frustrated than fulfilled. The egoist is sometimes shrewdly practical, but even then his approach is subjective; for his ends are always selfish and his calculations often misfire for want of real insight into the subjectivity of other people. The egoist does not regard his fellows as beings who are objective to himself and at the same time subjects in their own right, but (if he is not completely indifferent to them) he regards them either as extensions of himself or as objects to be manipulated in the same way in which things are manipulated. This often brings great suffering to those who are so regarded; for not only do they find their own purposes frustrated, but also their sense of their own selfhood is challenged, and they feel dehumanized or depersonalized.

The subjective relation of self to the world, then, is morally unsatisfactory in terms both of ethics and of personal satisfaction. The comfortable illusions with which the egoist surrounds himself may at any moment be shattered; and since his egoism has cut him off from genuine contact with the world and his fellows, he will, if disillusioned, have no relief from his loneliness and despair. He will have no ideal loyalties or intense interest in things outside of self to give life value in the absence of personal gratification. The claims which the egoist makes for himself can never be satisfied, and he may find the world to be a dull, drab, frustrating place.

Man is innately egoistic and it is natural for the mind initially to view all things as extensions of or related to the self; but it is equally natural for experience to make clear to the individual the disparity between the self and the non-self. The discovery of the otherness of things and people comes in many ways, all of them painful, though in varying degrees. And there are many responses to this experience. Some characters are destroyed by it; some are ennobled by their suffering; some are affected only momentarily; and some fly back to subjectivity, seeking an opiate by which they can escape pain and retain their sense of selfhood.

Man has a powerful need for a response to his consciousness, for a humanized world. The world of things is humanized by the individual's identification of himself with objects and places, by associations and long familiarity. But the chief humanizing agencies are society and other individuals; for in society and in our fellows we find objects which are endowed with consciousness (or are the products of consciousness) and which mediate between our consciousness and the completely alien, unconscious world of physical nature. Feuerbach contends that consciousness of the world is consciousness of the limitations of our own ego, and that we cannot pass directly from our initial egoistic state to an awareness of the world without introducing, preluding, and moderating "this contradiction by the consciousnes of a being who is indeed another, and in so far gives me the perception of my limitation, but in such a way as at the same time to affirm my own nature, make my nature objective to me." The consciousness of the world "is a humiliating consciousness . . . ; but the first stone against which the pride of egoism stumbles is the *thou,* the *alter ego.* The *ego* first steels its glance in the eye of a *thou* before it endures the contemplation of a being which does not reflect its own image . . . I reconcile myself with the world only through my fellow-man. Without other men, the world would be for me not only dead and empty, but meaningless" (*Essence,* p. 82).

The three ways in which self relates to the world are often, in the order presented, also stages of moral development through which Eliot's characters go in the process of maturation. The inevitable awakening to the disparity between the inward and the outward is frequently a source of moral growth; it makes clear to the individual the real relations of things and is the baptism of sorrow which renders him capable of true sympathy and fellowship. It makes him a sharer in the common lot; and, if it does not drive him back into illusion or into an embittered, defensive egoism, it nurtures in him the vision and sympathy necessary for the highest human fellowship. In the third stage of moral development, the individual's painful sense of the world's independent, alien existence is moderated by his vision of his connection with his fellow men and by his awareness of other human beings as subjective objects. He is moved, often, by an identification with and enthusiasm for groups and ends which transcend his individual existence; and his life-purpose becomes not primarily the pursuit of personal gratification but the achievement of genuine significance through living for others. This, for George Eliot, is the true religious life. The individual's feeling of solidarity with his fellows gives him a sense of religious orientation in the cosmos.

III

We are now, I think, in a position to see clearly the outcome of George Eliot's quest for values in a Godless universe—the quest in which she employed her novels as experiments in life. There are two orders—the cosmic and the moral—and we approach them in two ways, objectively and subjectively. Each order must be viewed with the proper combination of objectivity and subjectivity if we are to have both truth and value. Eliot rejected the subjective approach as a means of arriving at truth about the nature of the world, but she felt it to be the only way of comprehending the significance of human values, which, after all, have their origin in personal consciousness. But even when we deal with values, objectivity is important, for if we are to see values as having an external sanction, an existence apart from our own feelings, we must be able to relate to other men objectively, to see them as subjective objects, as they are for themselves as well for us.

The cosmic order must be viewed objectively, scientifically, if we are to have a knowledge of it which will enable us to adapt ourselves to it and it to our purposes. When the cosmic order is seen in an entirely subjective way—from the point of view of religion or metaphysics—the world is not seen truly and the mitigation of human ills through intelligent control of nature is impossible. When man projects his own consciousness into the cosmic order, making it in this way a moral order, the result is morality without truth—illusory, often pernicious morality.

On the other hand, a completely objective view of the cosmic order, although it yields truth, provides no morality. Without objectivity there is no truth; but without subjectivity, personal consciousness, there is no human value or meaning. Science is amoral, impersonal; it seeks to know the relations which objects bear to each other, and in order to do this it must deliberately suppress the subjective principle, as far as possible, and ignore the effects which external conditions have upon human goals and satisfactions. When external objects are seen only as they are related to each other, and not as they are related to the needs of the heart, they have no human, moral meaning.

When the cosmic order is seen from a purely subjective point of view, it is a comfortable home for the human spirit. Since the subjective principle is found to be the innermost essence of reality, the whole cosmos evidences the importance of man and sanctions his thoughts, feelings, and institutions. The objective point of view convinces us, however, that man's desire for absolute, immediate power over the course of things can never be fulfilled. Man and the cosmos are not in harmony; there is a disparity between the inward and the outward which can never be eliminated. The cosmos becomes, for the human spirit, an alien place, devoid of meaning and of love.

Objective knowledge of the cosmic order disappoints many of our hopes, but it also gives us a measure of security and allays a number of our fears. It gives us a real rather than an imagined power over the course of things. Knowledge mediates between man and the alienness of the cosmos by bringing the world into the domain of mind. To understand is, in a sense, to possess, to humanize. The cosmos is indifferent to man, but through knowledge man can envisage the cosmos and create within it a world of his own.

The cosmic order, no matter how it is viewed, cannot provide a true source or sanction of human values. Although an objective knowledge of the cosmic order enables us to serve moral ends by mitigating the painful disparity between the inward and the outward, only human feeling can determine the ends which this knowledge should be used to serve. But it is futile to *begin* our search for the moral implications of the cosmic order by addressing it from a predominantly personal point of view. With respect to the cosmic order, George Eliot reconciles truth and value by combining the objective and the subjective points of view. Her procedure is to view the cosmos first objectively, as it is presented by science, and then, without losing sight of its true, autonomous being, to seek its moral implications by regarding it from the subjective point of view, as it affects human destiny. The order of things cannot give value; but when it is seen from the human point of view, as it affects and can be affected by the moral order, it has great significance for morality.[13]

We have seen that when the cosmic order is viewed in a completely subjective manner it is made into an illusory moral order. On the other hand, when the human order is viewed objectively, from an external, impersonal point of view, moral values appear to be illusory. If we regard man, either the individual or the race, in terms of cosmic space and cosmic time, he is reduced to utter insignificance. When the individual sees himself in this way, he says, like Tolstoy's Konstantin Levin, "In infinite time, in infinite matter, in infinite space, is formed a bubble-organism, and that bubble lasts a while and bursts, and that bubble is me." [14] Eliot felt the objective view of man to be important in that it checks our egoism; thinking too highly of our own importance in the scheme of things leads to perpetual dissatisfaction and callousness towards others. She did not, however, regard man as unimportant. The objective view of man must be tempered by the subjective view, the view which recognizes human feelings and achievements as supremely important in their own sphere. The fact that when it is viewed in terms of cosmic time the span of a

13. For some of the moral implications that Eliot found in the cosmology of science, see my article "Science and Art in George Eliot's Quest for Values," *The Humanist*, XX (1960), 47–52.

14. *Anna Karenina*, Modern Library ed., p. 917.

human life appears infinitesimal need not, should not, and by and large, Eliot argued, does not affect man's sense of the importance of human endeavors, pleasures, and pains, or his sense of the significance of moral ideals. If human life is felt to be important by human beings, then to them it is important. What difference does the relative shortness of human existence make, Eliot asked Mrs. Ponsonby, *"when you have to consider the value of human experience"* (VI, 100)? The shortness of our lives does not lessen our intense concern that our existence be as satisfying as possible.

From the objective point of view the human order is seen to be a part of the mechanistic cosmic process. Man's behavior is determined by the blind forces at work both without and within. The individual appears to be the helpless pawn of heredity and environment. Intellectual and emotional processes, moral impulses and satisfactions, are reduced to physiological states and sequences. George Eliot insisted upon the importance and validity of man's subjective experience of himself. Objective analysis of mental and moral phenomena is extremely useful and interesting, but it should not prejudice our attitude towards the subjective, the felt aspects of experience. To regard human thought and feeling, pleasure and pain, as matters of little significance because of their physiological basis is, Eliot contended, "equivalent to saying that you care no longer for colour, now you know the laws of the spectrum" (VI, 98). Science had made Mrs. Ponsonby feel that moral endeavor is futile by denying the traditional conception of the freedom of the will. Eliot, after pointing out that the doctrine of determinism which ought logically to petrify our volition in fact makes little difference in how we feel or act, replied that

the consideration of molecular physics is not the direct ground of human love and moral action, any more than it is the direct means of composing a noble picture or of enjoying great music. One might as well hope to dissect one's own body and be merry in doing it, as take molecular physics (in which you must banish from your field of view what is specifically human) to be your dominant guide, your determiner of motives, in what is solely human. That every study has its bearing on every other is true; but pain and relief, love and sorrow, have their peculiar history which make an experience and knowledge over and above the swing of atoms (VI, 98–99).

Martin Svaglic, in his essay on "Religion in the Novels of George Eliot," asks, "if men are not free, why write books proposing virtue as a way of life?" [15] George Eliot was a thorough determinist whose moral philosophy was based upon the conviction that moral education, like the sciences of sociology and psychology, is possible only because man's actions are not the products of an arbitrary free will. Although she did not believe that man has free will (in the sense of absolute, uncaused volition), Eliot did believe that the individual has the ability to choose the better over the worse course if his motive and determination (themselves products of antecedent causes) are powerful enough. Her aim as a moralist was to initiate causes which would supply motive and strengthen determination. Thus there is no real inconsistency with her determinism in her exhortation to Mrs. Ponsonby to exert her will: "every fresh morning," she wrote, "is an opportunity that one can look forward to for exerting one's will. I shall not be satisfied with your philosophy till you have conciliated necessitarianism—I hate the ugly word—with the practise of willing strongly, willing to will strongly, and so on, that being what you certainly can do and have done about a great many things in life, whence it is clear that there is nothing in truth to hinder you from it—except you will say the absence of a motive. But that absence I don't believe in, in your case—only in the case of empty barren souls" (VI, 166). It appears that as a moralist Eliot felt a rigid belief in determinism to be dangerous if it issues (as it had for Mrs. Ponsonby) in a feeling of enslavement which can poison motive and diminish moral energy. But it is clear that Eliot held it possible to conciliate necessitarianism with the practice of willing strongly, and that she attacked not the truth of the law of universal causation but the possible psychological effects of a belief in it.

Closely connected with the issue of free will and determinism is, of course, the question of whether or not men are morally responsible for their actions. How, it may be asked, can Eliot construct and teach an ethic if she does not believe in free will and

15. *JEPG*, LII (1954), p. 149, ftn. 14. For a defense of Eliot's determinism, see George Levine, "Determinism and Responsibility in the Works of George Eliot," *PMLA*, LXXVII (1962), 268–279. Mr. Levine and I have arrived, independently, at similar conclusions.

hence cannot hold men morally responsible for their deeds? Eliot
never discusssed this problem (it seems not to have bothered her),
but she clearly could not have theoretically held men responsible
for their actions without contradicting her own philosophy; for
when human behavior is viewed objectively or scientifically it is
seen to be the product of external and internal conditions which
the individual cannot possibly choose for himself. The fact that
Eliot is sympathetic towards almost all her characters, including
many whom she finds morally deficient, suggests that she did in
fact feel them to be largely, if not entirely, the victims of circumstances and of their own inborn natures. But Eliot does not preach
that to understand all is to forgive all; and she does judge the
behavior of her characters. She presents their actions as blameworthy
and noble, and she expects the reader to share empathically the
character's sense of guilt or virtue. As a realist Eliot recognized that
men are not morally responsible for their actions; but as a moralist
who based her practice upon the findings of psychology, she felt
that moral judgment of past actions can have a potent influence
upon future behavior. For the purposes of morality, the individual
should be made to feel responsible for acts which he can be
educated to desist from or to repeat in the future. A sense of moral
responsibility and of the potency of his own will is not difficult to
inculcate in the individual, for it accords far better from his subjective experience of himself than do the doctrines of determinism
and freedom from responsibility, which are highly objective and
theoretical interpretations of experience. The important thing for
ethics is that we *feel* responsible and we *feel* free and that these feelings have a potent influence upon our behavior.

Given the fact that the moral order is not sustained by anything outside of itself, how can human values be said to have
objective validity? Is there any standard of value other than personal whim, taste, or conviction? Personal values, like orthodox
values, are satisfactory as long as they are not shattered by experience. But the individual has no security in the values which
he assigns to his own actions and existence, for these values change
with his moods and his fortunes. Even if he is fortunate, there
is always before him the prospect of death which annihilates his
own value-giving subjectivity and makes his satisfactions appear

transitory and insignificant. Man therefore craves something outside of himself, something which is not affected by the fluctuating pleasures and pains of his own experience and which endures beyond the term of his own life, to give indubitable significance to his being. George Eliot finds a subjective sanction of morality in the feelings of the individual and an objective sanction of morality in the feelings of other men, of humanity. Her insistence upon other men as the objective sanction of morality and upon living for others at its end is the rock, as it were, upon which Eliot's religion of humanity is built.

George Eliot's morality is grounded upon human subjectivity, but it is not, therefore, entirely subjective; or it is only so, logically, when mankind is considered as a single subject. Mankind as a subject has no object to which it can meaningfully relate or from which it can derive value; but to the individual, other men are significant objects, objective sources of value. Other men are significant objects to me because they have a consciousness akin to my own. To the individual, his fellows are separate, objectively existing beings ("I am not you") who are, at the same time, similar to him in nature ("I am like you") and responsive to his own inner life. In religion man finds value by making his own subjectivity objective to himself (God is a source of value only because he is a subjective object), but the subjective object from which he derives his morality has no external reality—other, Feuerbach would add, than in the species. But other men are to the individual subjective objects—and therefore objective sources of value—which do exist outside of the individual consciousness. And other men will continue to exist and to feel his influence after he is dead.

The primal, undeniable ground of value for Eliot is the individual's importance to himself; it is a fact that his own pleasures and pains are of great moment to him. This is the subjective basis of morality. The objective basis of morality is other men; and we become aware of it only when we regard our fellows objectively, that is, as subjects in themselves to whom we are objects. If I am important to myself, and other men have an inner life like my own, then they must be important to themselves. I evaluate the actions of my fellows in terms of the effects which they have upon me. Similarly, they must evaluate my actions by the effects which I have upon them. Other men, then, give my deeds, my life, an objective value. The moral satisfaction that we derive from living for the good of others is dependent upon the degree to which we regard our fellow-men objectively, upon our ability to project ourselves imaginatively into the consciousness of others and into the future. By living for others, we also live in others, and by envisioning the effects of our existence upon those who live after us we can experience a sense of impersonal immortality. "I think it is possible," Eliot wrote, "for this sort of impersonal life to attain great intensity" (V, 107).

If we live for others, as well as for ourselves, we will have a sense of the indubitable worth of our lives, a worth which is independent of the course of our personal fortunes. George Eliot assured Alexander Main that "amid all the considerable trials of existence, men and women can nevertheless greatly help each other; and while we can help each other it is worth while to live" (V, 358). If we are very fortunate we may find personal happiness; but whether we are happy or not, Eliot contends, we can lead meaningful lives by contributing to the happiness of others and by relieving their suffering. This is what Dorothea Brooke learns, this is what sustains her: "If we had lost our own chief good," she tells Will Ladislaw, "other people's good would remain and that is worth trying for. Some can be happy. I seemed to see that more clearly than ever, when I was the most wretched. I can hardly think how I could have borne the trouble, if that feeling had not come to me to make strength" (*Middlemarch,* Ch. LXXXIII). Romola too, like many other characters in Eliot's novels, comes to feel life's meaning in this way. In the plague-stricken village, removed from the complexities and intrigues of Florentine life which had obscured her sense of duty, Romola experiences the elemental fellowship with suffering which gives a life of service an indisputable, directly apprehended meaning: "If everything else is doubtful, this suffering that I can help is certain: if the glory of the cross is an illusion, the sorrow is only the truer" (Ch. LXIX).

The Authority of
the Past in
George Eliot's Novels

by Thomas Pinney

There are various ways of dividing George Eliot's work and of judging the parts it falls into. It was once the fashion to separate the novels based on recollected personal experience—*Scenes of Clerical Life, Adam Bede, The Mill on the Floss,* and *Silas Marner* —from the more labored *Romola, Felix Holt, Middlemarch,* and *Daniel Deronda,* and to call the first group novels of "feeling" and therefore good, the second, novels of "intellect" and, therefore, inferior. Later comment, following the lead of F. R. Leavis especially, has silently accepted these lines of division but reversed the judgment: the novels of feeling, it is said, are flawed by sentimental indulgence, the novels of intellect alone are mature. *Middlemarch* and *Daniel Deronda* now receive more admiring attention than all the other novels together. Recently, Miriam Allott has suggested a kind of three-part division between the fresh and spontaneous novels through *Silas Marner,* the arid *Romola* and *Felix Holt,* and the mature *Middlemarch* and *Deronda.*[1] Then there are the patterns that can be constructed by following out any one of an indefinite number of developing tendencies in her novels. *Scenes of Clerical Life, Adam Bede, Silas Marner*—perhaps *The*

"The Authority of the Past in George Eliot's Novels" by Thomas Pinney. From *Nineteenth-Century Fiction,* XXI, No. 2 (September, 1966), 131–47. Copyright © 1966 by The Regents of the University of California. Reprinted by permission of the author and The Regents.

1. "George Eliot in the 1860's" *Victorian Studies,* V (Dec., 1961), 93–108.

Mill on the Floss—are distinguished from the others by their use of unheroic character. In the rest, George Eliot abandons the effort to construct tragedy around an inarticulate and imperfectly self-conscious character and turns instead to studies of greater complexity, culminating in the figures of Dorothea and Gwendolen. Or, the line may be drawn according to the attitude towards evil shown in the novels: the optimistic assumptions of *Adam Bede* and *Silas Marner* disappear, to be replaced by the melancholy of *Middlemarch* and *Deronda*. It should be said that George Eliot herself gave the first hint for dividing her work in this dramatic fashion. According to J. W. Cross, in his *Life* of George Eliot, she told him that "she could put her finger on" the writing of *Romola* "as marking a well-defined transition in her life. In her own words, 'I began it a young woman,—I finished it an old woman.' " [2] What she here says of her own life it has seemed reasonable to extend to the character of her novels.

Without claiming that it produces a division any less limited than the others, I think that a very striking development can be seen in *Daniel Deronda* that sets it clearly apart from George Eliot's other novels. To describe this change may also help to reveal the continuity of most of George Eliot's work in the very process of showing how, at the end, she took a new turn

George Eliot's mind was a mixture, though not a balance, of conservative and reforming tendencies. As Cross says in the *Life:*

> her roots were down in the pre-railroad, pre-telegraphic period—the days of fine old leisure—but the fruit was formed during an era of extraordinary activity in scientific and mechanical discovery. Her genius was the outcome of these conditions (I, 8–9).

The outcome of such conflicting tendencies was the "conservative-reforming" tension so admirably analyzed by Basil Willey,[3] but of the two elements the conservative was consistently the stronger. The way in which her novels mingle respect for the new with tenderness for the old is typified by a passage from *The Mill on the Floss:*

2. *George Eliot's Life*, Cabinet ed., II, 300. Unless otherwise noted, all quotations from George Eliot's works are from this edition.
3. *Nineteenth-Century Studies* (London, 1949), chs. 8 and 9.

is not the striving after something better and better in our surround-
ings, the grand characteristic that distinguishes man from the brute ... ?
But heaven knows where that striving might lead us, if our affections
had not a trick of twining round those old inferior things—if the loves
and sanctities of our life had no deep immovable roots in memory
(Book 2, ch. 1).

The various tones of the passage are a key to George Eliot's mind.
The self-conscious rhetoric of "the grand characteristic that distinguishes man from the brute" creates a mild irony, but this critical hint is balanced by the admission that our affections play a
"trick" in clinging to things not only "old" but confessedly "inferior." After that, however, the shift of tone to the seriousness of
"loves and sanctities" and "deep immovable roots" weights the
passage in favor of the conservative impulse. The gentle bias this
extract displays in favor of the conservative affections might be
paralleled by many illustrations from the novels. To take only a
few of the more obvious points, all except one of the novels are
set in a past at least one generation removed from the time of their
composition—most often the period chosen is the time of George
Eliot's childhood. The novels are full of loving description of old
manners and ways of life, and describe charitably even those things
from the past that George Eliot's mind recognized as imperfect,
backward, or obstructive. *Felix Holt* and *Middlemarch,* which deal
directly with the era of the Reform Bill, show through their sustained and searching criticism of the motives, possibilities, and
effects of the reform movement George Eliot's refusal to accept
the doctrine of assured progress. It is significant that the political
and social reforms approved in the novels turn out to be not innovation but restoration, like Felix Holt's attempt to bring about
the moral regeneration of the working men,[4] or Deronda's dedica-
tion to the cause of Zionism. Even Lydgate's advanced scientific
ideas are based on the principle of the organic interdependence of
life, a new conception in scientific research but a commonplace of
conservatism in social thought.

The woman of enlightened opinion who broke with the Church,

4. "Felix Holt the Radical is rather Felix Holt the Conservative; he is not
even a Tory-Democrat" (Joseph Jacobs, *Literary Studies* [London, 1895], p. xxi).

translated Strauss and Feuerbach, and edited the *Westminster Review* had her part in writing the novels: their liberal and sympathetic point of view, their interest in the problems of reform, and their wide range of allusion to the concerns of contemporary science and philosophy are enough to show this. Nevertheless, the chief values of the novels are on the whole conservative, cherishing what is known and familiar, seeking the good in outmoded forms, and remaining skeptical of all hopes for swift and inevitable progress. When George Eliot wrote to one of her correspondents that "the bent of my mind is conservative" she appealed to her novels for the proof of her description.[5]

The basis of George Eliot's conservatism was a piety towards her early experience that grew out of affection, imagination, and reverence rather than formal argument. But she was a conservative through a reasoned analysis of human society, too. As she wrote in her review of Riehl's *Natural History of German Life:*

> What has grown up historically can only die out historically, by the gradual operation of necessary laws. The external conditions which society has inherited from the past are but the manifestations of inherited internal conditions in the human beings who compose it. . . . The nature of European man has its roots intertwined with the past.[6]

This was the view she held throughout the creative period of her life; it is affirmed again in a letter written in the year of her death: "the reason societies change slowly is, because individual men and women cannot have their natures changed by doctrine and can only be wrought on by little and little" (*Letters*, VII, 346). The symbol and expression of human nature is language: a slow, complex, cumulative growth that George Eliot describes by quoting Wordsworth—"familiar with forgotten years." [7]

5. *The George Eliot Letters,* ed. Gordon S. Haight, 7 vols. (New Haven, 1954–1955), IV, 472.

6. *Westminster Review*, LXVI, 69–70.

7. In the essay on Riehl, *Westminster Review*, LXVI, 69. The line is from *The Excursion,* I, 276, and was apparently a favorite of George Eliot's as an expression of her notion of the organic relation of past to present. She quotes it again in *The Mill on the Floss,* Book 1, ch. 12, to describe the town of St. Ogg's and its still vital connection with "the thoughts and hands of widely-sundered generations."

The passage from her essay on Riehl, with its analogy between man's relation to his past and the plant rooted in its sustaining soil, places George Eliot in the English tradition of "emotional naturalism," [8] stemming from Burke, and passing through Wordsworth and Scott. Whatever is abstract, rational, and general is, in this view, bound to be misguided, because alien to the real requirements of human nature. Only by consulting what is concrete, imaginative, and particular, can one hope to understand man, and to prescribe for him. Like Wordsworth's Wanderer, George Eliot had been taught by history and by "nature's gradual processes" [9] to distrust all abstract schemes, and to reverence the life of the past as a guide for the present.

At the heart of each of George Eliot's novels lies the conviction that the basis of morality, and hence the vital principle of all that is good in life, is strength of feeling. Adam Bede's simple expression of this doctrine—"It isn't notions sets people doing the right thing—it's feelings" (*Adam Bede*, ch. 17)—is exemplified with more or less complexity in all of George Eliot's work, and is no less important in her last than in her first novel. In the light of this belief in the moral supremacy of feeling George Eliot's conservatism is best understood. Old and familiar objects and associations are cherished not because they possess a necessarily superior intrinsic value, but because they have drawn to themselves those affections which supply all the meaning of life, and have become inseparable from the feelings which exalt them. The affections, because freshest and most intense in our early life, are inevitably backward looking. Not what is to come but what has been determines the values that guide action. For this reason the strong and sympathetic characters in the novels are always shown as full of reverent piety towards their known and familiar world. The following passage from *Romola* is typical:

> Again she felt that there could be no law for her but the law of her affections. That tenderness and keen fellow-feeling for the near and the loved, which are the main outgrowth of the affections, had made the religion of her life (ch. 36).

8. The phrase is Basil Willey's, *The Eighteenth Century Background* (New York and London, 1941), p. 211.
9. *The Excursion*, IV, 288.

Romola's conviction is later shown to be inadequate as the sole guide to conduct, since the law of duty may cut across the law of affection. But the ideal moral position frequently illustrated in the novels is that in which the laws of duty and affection coincide.[10]

The identification of the "law of . . . affections" with "religion" may seem extravagant, but the evidence of the novels shows that George Eliot means it seriously. *Romola* is an especialy clear illustration of the religion of feeling in action, perhaps because George Eliot, in writing a story so remote from her own experience, works out her meaning in situations and actions more abstractly conceived than is usual in her novels. Every one of Romola's actions is determined by the authority of her feelings: this is the consistent principle that reconciles the apparent contradictions of her life. Her dutiful apprenticeship in classical learning is only the expression of filial tenderness, and the novel makes much of the contrast between the aridity of Romola's studies and the intensity of feeling that prompts them: "all Romola's ardour had been concentrated in her affections. Her share in her father's learned pursuits had been for her little more than a toil which was borne for his sake" (ch. 27). Romola's "conversion" to Christianity from the pagan skepticism derived from her father is no more an intellectual act than her earlier classical studies had been but, like them, an expression of her emotional attachment to the man whose example sways her—in this case, Savonarola. Earlier, when her brother has attempted to warn her against marriage with Tito, he has failed because his prophetic vision seemed to Romola to come from the "shadowy region where human souls seek wisdom apart from the human sympathies which are the very life and substance of our wisdom." He should have appealed instead to "filial and brotherly affection" (ch. 15). When Savonarola's reforming zeal, like old Bardo's zeal for Greek learning, comes into conflict with human feeling, Romola turns from Christianity. Her re-

10. It would be more precise to say that passion rather than affection may conflict with duty. Where love is not enough, the love in question is usually an explosive outbreak rather than the slowly accumulated growth of affection. The distinction is illustrated in Maggie's refusal to run off with Stephen Guest: her feeling for him is an overwhelming passion which runs athwart all her established loyalties. She sees her duty in choosing to remain "true to my calmer affections" *(The Mill on the Floss,* Book 6, ch. 14).

lapse involves no intellectual distress: "She had appropriated no theories: she had simply felt strong in the strength of affection" (ch. 36). Her perplexities are not intellectual difficulties, but arise from a hopeless conflict of pious loyalties—to her father, to Savonarola (his addressing Romola always as "my daughter" is not merely a conventional form to her), and to her godfather, Bernardo del Nero. Only when the objects of these competing loyalties—her three "fathers"—have disappeared from Romola's life can she find an untroubled peace in an unquestioning life of devoted human service. George Eliot's description of Romola's restoration to a life of undivided affection heavily stresses the fact that it comes about independently of the mind. Romola is simply allowed to fall back on her affections in nursing the plague-stricken villagers, and her life comes whole again. "She had not even reflected," George Eliot writes; "she had simply lived"; her work is "impulse," not "argument," and she finds "new baptism" through her spontaneous participation in "the simpler relations of the human being to his fellow-men." [11]

At times George Eliot seems content to let the affections stand as their own justification: what is loved is good precisely and solely because it is loved, or, as she writes in *Romola,* "every strong feeling makes to itself a conscience of its own—has its own piety" (ch. 34). But her religion of feeling does allow distinctions: not all objects of affection are equally good, and affections may be misplaced. A recurrent problem in the novels is the question of rebellion. What should a person do if he feels, or thinks he feels, that the world of his familiar associations, and hence the world that claims his first affections, is mean and cramping? Maggie Tulliver is especially troubled by the tension between her critical judgment of the society that includes the Pullets and Gleggs, symbols of provincial narrowness, and her tenderness for the other part of that society in which all her most intimate loyalties are set—to her father, to the mill, to her childhood with Tom, to Lucy, and to Philip. At the moment of her great crisis of decision she recognizes that her early affections must determine the conduct of her life: "If the past is

11. Ch. 69. Compare the last phrase with George Eliot's description of the theme of *Silas Marner:* "the remedial influences of pure, natural human relations" (*Letters,* III, 382).

not to bind us, where can duty lie? We should have no law but the inclination of the moment" (*Mill on the Floss,* Book 6, ch. 14). Her love for Stephen is no answer to her question, and Maggie submits to her past, knowing that the pain of renunciation is the price of righteousness. The past that Maggie has known is by no means perfect, yet it derives, through its hold on the affections, an authority superior to every new claim in her life. And, whatever else one may make of the ending of the novel, its intention is clearly to affirm the supreme value of the early affection of Maggie and Tom for each other: they are joined by "deep, underlying unshakable memories of early union" (Book 7, ch. 5).

Still, piety may have to recognize that it has been mistaken about its object. Romola is right to rebel against Tito and Savonarola; Dorothea is right to resist Casaubon's attempt to control her life even after his death; Mirah is right not to obey her disreputable father. But these are exceptional cases, in which genuine feeling has been deceived into spending itself on unworthy persons. The things that are shown as capable of supporting a lasting affection are relatively few, implying that they do not owe all their virtue to the fact that they are loved, but that they are rightly loved. It may be the memory of some virtuous and loving person, as it is in "Amos Barton" and "Janet's Repentance"; it may be, as it most often is, the family and the familiar scenes and associations of childhood or youth, as in *Silas Marner, The Mill on the Floss, Felix Holt,* and *Middlemarch;* or it may be an idea of service, growing out of human sympathy, as in *Romola* and *Daniel Deronda.*

Because affection for the near and familiar is so important as a source of value, it is essential for the novels to make us understand and sympathize with the objects of that affection. No novelist before George Eliot shows his characters so deeply attached to places, and to particular ways of life, so intimately linked by association to a familiar world that the preservation of the relation, whether in memory or in fact, becomes the condition of life itself. The idea is made explicit in such a passage as this, from *Daniel Deronda:*

A human life, I think, should be well-rooted in some spot of a native land, where it may get the love of tender kinship for the face of the earth, for the labours men go forth to, for the sounds and accents that haunt it . . . a spot where the definiteness of early memories may be inwrought with affection . . . may spread not by sentimental effort and reflection, but as a sweet habit of the blood (ch. 3).

The strength and freshness of the child's sensibilities give to early associations a power no later attachment can equal. With this conviction the narrator of *The Mill on the Floss* argues against those "severely regulated minds who are free from the weakness of any attachment that does not rest on a demonstrable superiority of qualities." His own preferences are supported by "early memory": the vulgar elderberry bush is hallowed because "it is no novelty in my life, speaking to me merely through my present sensibilities to form and colour, but the long companion of my existence, that wove itself into my joys when joys were vivid" (Book 2, ch. 1). Catherina loves Mr. Bates's home, Mosslands, because "every object in it, every sound that haunted it, had been familiar to her from the days when she had been carried thither on Mr. Bates's arm" ("Mr. Gilfil's Love Story," ch. 7). The inseparability of the Poyser family from the farm that has been passed down from father to son, Elizabeth Bede's determination to be buried under the white hawthorne tree in the churchyard, Mr. Tulliver's affection for his mill, all illustrate the "feelings of inheritance, home, and personal and family independence" that Wordsworth dramatized in "Michael." [12] Tulliver, after he has been sold up, consents to stay on at the mill under the hated Wakem's authority because his life-long association with the place has made him literally inseparable from it:

> He couldn't bear to think of himself living on any other spot than this, where he knew the sound of every gate and door, and felt that the shape and colour of every roof and weather-stain and broken hillock was good, because his growing senses had been fed on them . . . and where life seemed like a familiar smooth-handled tool that the fingers clutch with loving ease (*Mill on the Floss*, Book 3, ch. 9).

In *Middlemarch*, as Fred and Rosamond ride over to Stone Court through the morning fields, the narrative pauses to describe

> a pretty bit of midland landscape, almost all meadows and pastures, with hedgerows still allowed to grow in bushy beauty and to spread out

12. *Early Letters of William and Dorothy Wordsworth (1787–1805)*, ed. E. de Selincourt (Oxford, 1935), p. 266.

coral fruit for the birds. Little details gave each field a particular physiognomy, dear to the eyes that have looked on them from child-hood. . . . These are the things that make the gamut of joy in landscape to midland-bred souls—the things they toddled among, or perhaps learned by heart standing between their father's knees while he drove leisurely.[13]

If George Eliot agrees with Wordsworth that the experiences of childhood are the "root of piety," establishing what is to be best and dearest in future years, she also shares his concern with the problem of maintaining the continuity of that experience, to find

> the ties
> That bind the perishable hours of life
> Each to the other, and the curious props
> By which the world of memory and thought
> Exists and is sustained (*The Prelude*, VII, 460–465).

The solution to the problem, for both George Eliot and Words-worth, lies in the virtue of piety, understood as the spirit that pre-serves the oneness of the individual consciousness and cherishes as a sacred inheritance the good in our past months and years. The only healthy growth springs from the root of piety; as George Eliot writes in *The Spanish Gypsy:*

> The only better is a Past that lives
> On through an added Present, stretching still
> In hope unchecked by shaming memories
> To life's last breath (Book 1, p. 111).

In Wordsworth, two forces sustain piety. The first is the world of natural objects, standing as perpetual reminders of the experiences associated with them; the second is memory, recalling those "spots

13. Ch. 12. There is a strong family resemblance between the scenes of natural beauty George Eliot describes, in her novels and elsewhere, sufficient to define her taste in the matter. Compare the scenes described in the passage from *Mid-dlemarch* with those in "Brother and Sister," *The Mill on the Floss*, the Intro-duction to *Felix Holt, Daniel Deronda*, and the "Looking Backward" chapter of *Theophrastus Such*, in which the same details recur. In the *Middlemarch* pas-sage, the meaning of the observation that the hedgerows are "still allowed to grow in bushy beauty" is explained in the description of unreformed England in the Introduction to *Felix Holt*. Before Reform, "everywhere the bushy hedge-rows wasted the land with their straggling beauty." Reform gets rid of the waste, but at the expense of the beauty. The description is an expression in detail of George Eliot's mixed attitudes.

of time" of pre-eminent imaginative power, and by recreating the conditions of those past moments, reawakening imagination itself. In this manner "feeling comes in aid / Of feeling . . . if but once we have been strong." [14] Wordsworth's interest in the "props" of memory is egocentric, a concern to obtain proofs of the soul's power in order to guarantee the soul's indestructibility. Memory is no less important in the psychology and morality of George Eliot's novels, but ideally her characters seek self-knowledge through memory in order to determine their duties no less than their privileges. In this sense, George Eliot's conception is closer than Wordsworth's to the Roman idea of *pietas*. In her characters, an active and untroubled memory is the infallible sign of moral health. Only those who enjoy "that unity which lies in the selection of our keenest consciousness" (*Middlemarch*, ch. 34) are strong against change, and the first effect of any serious dislocation is a break in the wholeness of memory, sometimes ending in its destruction. Whenever a person's life drifts into a course opposed to its early affections and aspirations, then the memory ceases to be "a temple where all relics and all votive offerings, all worship and all grateful joy, are an unbroken history sanctified by one religion" (*Felix Holt*, ch. 44).

The image George Eliot uses most often to express the idea of continuity in growth is the metaphor of the plant. The human personality is like a tree whose sustaining root is early experience, but the root can function only through the network of veins which is the memory, carrying nourishment to the remotest branches of the tree. In the language of this image, the memory is a "fibre," one of the most potent words in George Eliot's vocabulary. We read, for example, that "In the man whose childhood has known caresses there is always a fibre of memory that can be touched to gentle issues" ("Janet's Repentance," ch. 7). Or we find that the power of simple words and gestures lies in their "stirring the long-winding fibres of your memory, and enriching your present with your most precious past" (*Adam Bede*, ch. 50). In Tom Tulliver "there were tender fibers . . . that had been used to answer to Maggie's fondling" (*Mill on the Floss*, Book 1, ch. 5). Maggie's thought of Philip and Lucy "had stirred all the fibres that bound her to the calmer

14. *The Prelude*, XII, 269-271. The passage is one of those George Eliot marked in her copy of the poem, now in the Yale University Library.

past" (*Mill on the Floss,* Book 7, ch. 5). Silas Marner's is a "clinging life . . . though the object round which its fibres had clung was a dead disrupted thing"; so Silas grows "withered and shrunken" (*Silas Marner,* ch. 10). In *Romola,* we read of "living fibre . . . fed with the memory of familiar things" (ch. 69). Mrs. Transome is made to feel that "every fibre" in her is "a memory that makes a pang" (*Felix Holt,* ch. 39). And when Fred Vincy grows ill, "all the deepest fibres of [his] mother's memory were stirred" (*Middlemarch,* ch. 27).

The completest types of an ideal continuity in life arising from deeply-rooted affection and faithful performance of duty are Eppie and Mary Garth. Eppie is not a fully satisfactory guide to the conduct of life because her desires are so limited and the possibilities of action for her so restricted that she hardly knows what temptation and illusion are. Being planted in one spot, her affections are so thoroughly grown around her familiar world that the chance to remove to another world is a threat rather than a temptation. She and Marner are grown together so that to separate them would, as Marner says, "cut us in two" (*Silas Marner,* ch. 19).

Mary Garth, unlike Eppie, has an active intellect as well as strong feelings; for her, loyalty and duty may involve the sacrifice of possibilities that she is intelligent enough to see lying open to her. But she never doubts that her memories and affections define duty for her and determine the conditions of good in her life. Farebrother's love for her is, unlike most of the temptations that beset George Eliot's heroines, neither illusory nor inferior in value to the thing already possessed, since Farebrother is clearly superior as a man to Fred Vincy. The significant difference between Mary's two lovers is not any intrinsic difference, however; it is the difference in their relation to her past. "She had never thought that any man could love her except Fred, who had espoused her with the umbrella ring, when she wore socks and little strapped shoes." As a result, Mary can say: "I should never be quite happy if I thought he was unhappy for the loss of me. It has taken such deep root in me—my gratitude to him for always loving me best." [15] Mary

15. *Middlemarch,* ch. 52. Compare Maggie's loyalty to Philip: though she is passionately attracted to Stephen, she would marry Philip because "he loved me first. No one else could be quite what he is to me" (*The Mill on the Floss,* Book 6, ch. 9).

knows what she gives up in Farebrother: "It was impossible to help fleeting visions of another kind—new dignities and an acknowledged value of which she had often felt the absence." At the same time her long-established relation to Fred is a law to her feelings:

> When a tender affection has been storing itself in us through many of our years, the idea that we could accept any exchange for it seems to be a cheapening of our lives. And we can set a watch over our affections and our constancy as we can over other treasures (*Middlemarch*, ch. 57).

In acting on this principle, Mary typifies a wisdom frequently illustrated in George Eliot's novels. Eppie's love for Marner, Maggie's loyalty to her past, Romola's piety towards her father, Esther's tenderness for Rufus Lyon, do not justify themselves by claiming any special virtue in their objects, though there is in the novels a discernible preference shown to humble, unpretentious, and unfashionable things. But the real authority behind such conduct is simply the existence of strong feeling for something known and loved. However great the improvement to be gained, from an intellectual or worldly point of view, by bargaining old loyalties for new, to do so is always wrong because it violates the duties laid down by piety and leads to self-division.

In the novels before *Daniel Deronda* the idea that the good in one's life has been determined by the past is clearly and most dramatically illustrated in such actions as Maggie's rejection of Stephen Guest, Eppie's rejection of Godfrey Cass, and Esther's rejection of Harold Transome. These are decisions made on the basis of loyalty to one's own intimate, private past as it appears in the light of affection. When we reach *Daniel Deronda*, however, and find the hero giving up his life as an English gentleman in order to devote himself to the service of his newly discovered Jewish people, we have encountered a new moral principle that is almost an inversion of the old one,[16] and that is to be explained, I think, as an instance of the Religion of Humanity transforming the more personal and Wordsworthian strain in George Eliot's work.

16. Deronda's decision does have in common with the choices of Maggie, Eppie, and Esther the element of self-denial—worldly advantage is refused in each case.

Deronda is, if you like, exhibiting piety in his choice to serve
the people to which he belongs, but it is a piety towards an abstract,
ideal past—an "inheritance" that has only an intellectual meaning.[17] The past determines duty for Deronda just as it does for
Maggie, with the significant difference that Deronda's is a "past"
he never had. If the abstract and legal conception of the past that
guides Deronda had been applied in the earlier novels, then Eppie
would have left Silas for Godfrey Cass, who was, after all, her
father, and hence the accredited recipient of her duty. For the same
reasons, Esther Lyon ought not to have left Transome Court to return to the world of Rufus Lyon and Felix Holt. Was she not the
legal heir to the position that Harold Transome offers her? Clearly,
in the earlier novels the authority of the past is inseparable from
the affections that grow out of personal experience; in *Daniel
Deronda,* it is not. The past in *Deronda* is not a private past, and
its authority depends not on affection but on some reasoned principle of inheritance and duty. In Comtean terms, Deronda is submitting himself to the principle of "continuity" or "filiation"—
the idea that his life is an organic part of the Jewish past and can
only be realized through the effort to serve the historic purposes of
that past. As Comte says:

> It is our filiation with the Past, even more than our connexion with
> the Present, which teaches us that the only real life is the collective
> life of the race; that individual life has no existence except as an
> abstraction. Continuity is the feature which distinguishes our race
> from all others. Many of the lower races are able to form a union
> among their living members; but it was reserved for Man to conceive
> and realize co-operation of successive generations, the source to which
> the gradual growth of civilization is to be traced.[18]

17. C. S. Lewis's definition of *pius* in classical Latin is relevant here: "some-
where between 'dutiful' and 'affectionate.' The man who is *pius* or 'kind' (in
this sense) is one who does not good offices in general, but good offices to which
close kinship or some other personal relationship binds him" (*Studies in Words*
[Cambridge, 1960], p. 30).

18. *A General View of Positivism,* trans. J. H. Bridges, Academic Reprints
(Stanford, California, n.d. [orig. 1865]), p. 404. George Eliot had reservations
about Comte's principle of continuity, as she did about most of his doctrines.
In a MS essay entitled "Historic Guidance" from a notebook that I am now
preparing for publication, she observes that since the life of the past inevitably
reveals a mixture of good and bad forces, continuity by itself is an insufficient

To account for the new concept of inherited duty exhibited in *Deronda,* I think we must suppose that George Eliot grew increasingly less certain of the "holiness of the heart's affections" for what is merely personal, and began to feel the necessity for some sanction to duty more philosophical and less subject to accident than the law of private affection. The past is still to bind us, but a past newly interpreted not as a living body of experience but as the sum of remote hereditary conditions.[19] Thus our loyalties are extended to include more than a single old weaver in Raveloe, or a brother in St. Ogg's; they must now be given to the service of a whole race. The change is away from direct personal relationships and towards the service of collective entities. The Comtean love of Humanity is too bloodless an abstraction to make a plausible motive, but I suspect that George Eliot meant Deronda's vision of the Jewish nation to be a dramatically acceptable equivalent to it.

The first indication that George Eliot no longer considers affection enough is to be found in *Romola.* There the heroine's desire to find some object to satisfy her need to love is answered by allowing her to minister to an entire village, and to rescue from distress the helpless Tessa and her children. The children, indeed, are Tito's, so that they are not unconnected with Romola's private past, but there is a suggestion of humanitarian service here that is absent from, say, Maggie's loyalty to Tom. Again, in *Felix Holt,* Esther's decision to remain faithful to her familiar world is not entirely based on the fact that it is her world and has made the past she loves. Felix means to serve the cause of reform, as Harold Transome does not, and by allying herself with Felix she devotes herself indirectly to an ideal of active public benevolence that helps to "justify" her affections.

The most doctrinaire example of George Eliot's later concept of piety and duty is not one of her novels, but her poem, *The Spanish Gypsy.* In it, the Religion of Humanity utterly destroys the

---

guide. But the rightness of the Jewish struggle for national identity is not questioned in *Deronda.*

19. Joseph Jacobs, who calls George Eliot the "literary voice of Darwinism," sees, rightly I think, a scientific influence on her treatment of the moral claims of heredity: "The leading conception of modern science as applied to man, the influence of hereditary transmission, was transmuted into the moral principle of the claims of race" (*Literary Studies,* pp. xxi; 8).

law of affection. Fedalma (originally Fidalma—the faithful soul) as a child was stolen from the Gypsies and has been brought up in the household of the Spanish Duchess Diana. She is betrothed to the Duchess's son, the Duke Silva, but on the eve of her marriage is visited by her father, the Gypsy prince Zarca, who exhorts her to return to her people and work for their establishment as an independent nation (the parallel with *Deronda* here is obvious). After a perfunctory struggle, Fedalma gives up her personal desires and assumes the role of leader of her people's destinies. The very plain moral of the tale is that private interests and private loyalties, no matter how blameless and genuine, are but a straw in the balance against the weighty claims of racial and public, or "inherited," duties.[20]

When George Eliot returned to the theme of *The Spanish Gypsy* in the Jewish part of *Daniel Deronda,* she was careful to avoid the most obvious dramatic and psychological implausibility of the poem. Fedalma's shift of loyalties from Don Silva to the Gypsies is offensive because her love for him has the whole of her personal history behind it and her relation to the Gypsies none. Thus her determination to give him up seems, if theoretically admirable, emotionally criminal, especially since the cause to which she sacrifices him is such a desperate enterprise.[21] Fedalma apparently denies the truth of the sentiment so characteristic of George Eliot's other heroines, that the abandonment of an affection of long standing in favor of a new is a betrayal of trust and an offense against the integrity of personality.

In *Daniel Deronda* the grounds for making this charge against the hero are carefully skirted by leaving him uncommitted until he discovers his heritage. Deronda grows up in the full consciousness of his separateness from the life around him, and has the

20. As Leslie Stephen says, Fedalma's doctrine "stated in cold blood, seems to be that our principles are to be determined by the physical fact of ancestry. . . . to throw overboard all other ties on the simple ground of descent, and adopt the most preposterous schemes of the vagabonds to whom you are related, seems to be very bad morality whatever may be its affinity to positivism" (*George Eliot* [New York and London, 1913], p. 166).

21. To George Eliot the very futility of Fedalma's enterprise made part of its heroic essence. See the section entitled " 'A Fine Excess.' Feeling is Energy" in *Essays and Leaves from a Note-Book,* pp. 307–309.

further assurance of knowing that none of the comfortable people among whom his life is lived really needs him. Though Gwendolen falls in love with him, his feeling for her is not so much love as sympathetic curiosity. When he turns his back on England and Gwendolen, then, he does not sacrifice a grand passion as Fedalma does. Besides, he is consoled with the lovely Mirah, whereas no romantic Gypsy prince is promised to Fedalma as she sails off with her people to Africa. For the rest, Deronda is at liberty to indulge an indiscriminate sympathy until such time as an authoritative claim on his loyalties shall be made. When he learns of his Jewish parentage, he is delighted at this deliverance from the paralysis of "impartial sympathy." Before the revelation he had lacked "that noble partiality which is man's best strength, the closer fellowship that makes sympathy practical." Now, committed to his Jewishness, Deronda is able to exchange "that bird's eye reasonableness which soars to avoid preference and loses all sense of quality, for the generous reasonableness of drawing shoulder to shoulder with men of like inheritance" (ch. 73).

It is difficult to avoid the conclusion that George Eliot is trying to have it both ways in this explanation of Deronda's choice. More charitably, we might say that in the hereditary claims of race Deronda resolves the conflict between the ideals of wide sympathy —"fellow-feeling"—and personal affection. He is allowed to have preferences and affections, but the danger that such things will result in narrow exclusiveness is neutralized by assigning him the widest possible preference—he will serve a whole race.

If much of George Eliot's earlier work shows strong affinities with Wordsworth, there is also a curious parallel between the development in George Eliot that led to *Daniel Deronda* and Wordsworth's own development. A fundamental reason for the resemblance between George Eliot and Wordsworth is the fact that both faced the world alone, without the support of the traditional religious explanations of man and the world. As Wordsworth was the first of poets to be "left . . . alone with the visible universe" so George Eliot is the "first great agnostic novelist." [22] Both of them are

22. Basil Willey, *The Seventeenth Century Background,* Anchor Books (Garden City, 1953), p. 300. Barbara Hardy, *The Novels of George Eliot* (London, 1959), p. 22.

seeking in their work to discover a principle of coherence and order that will give isolated man a sense of home in the world. Wordsworth himself, with advancing years, came more and more to look for support not in the declining power of feeling but in the English church and an ideal of the English nation—"the weight of all this unintelligible world" in time becomes too much for the unaided spirit to support alone. Like George Eliot's later position, Wordsworth's may be interpreted as an attempt to compromise between personal, heart-felt experience and the necessity for a more comprehensive, public authority. To the extent that his ideals of church and nation were English, they represented something to which he belonged by the closest ties of personal experience; but they also provided the external, formal support for faith and hope that the unmediated relation between his spirit and the world could no longer give by itself. George Eliot, in *Deronda,* has worked out much the same kind of compromise scheme for her hero, who gladly and with a sense of relief puts his faith in his people because they are *his* people, and also because they are greater than he is. Perhaps it is inevitable that a morality of pious affection should eventually require supports independent of personal experience, as the years weaken the strength of the feelings and call out the philosophic mind in their place. Such a development was Wordsworth's, and it might have been predicted from his example that George Eliot's morality of the heart's simple affections would at last lead to the conclusion of *Daniel Deronda.*

The Moment of Disenchantment
in George Eliot's Novels

by Barbara Hardy

In almost all George Eliot's novels there is a crisis of disenchantment described in images which echo, more or less closely, a passage in one of her letters. On 4 June 1848 she wrote to Sara Hennell:

> Alas for the fate of poor mortals which condemns them to wake up some fine morning and find all the poetry in which their world was bathed, only the evening before, utterly gone!—the hard, angular world of chairs and tables and looking-glasses staring at them in all its naked prose! [1]

This image of the disenchanted day-lit room is one of the most important recurring images in her work. It first returns in "Janet's Repentance" though in a context very different from that of George Eliot's lament. Janet's cold, hard vision of reality is no result of waking from a dream: it summarizes and freezes a disenchantment with which she has been living without fully admitting it:

> The daylight changes the aspect of misery to us, as of everything else. In the night it presses on our imagination—the forms it takes are false, fitful, exaggerated; in broad day it sickens our sense with the dreary persistence of definite measurable reality. . . . That moment of intensest depression was come to Janet, when the daylight which showed her the walls, and chairs, and tables, and all the

"The Moment of Disenchantment in George Eliot's Novels" by Barbara Hardy. From *The Review of English Studies*, New Series, V, No. 19 (July, 1954), 256–64. Copyright 1954 by The Clarendon Press. Reprinted by permission of The Clarendon Press, Oxford. A revised version appears in *The Novels of George Eliot* (London: The Athlone Press, 1959, 1963).

1. *George Eliot's Life as related in her Letters and Journals*, ed. J. W. Cross (London, 1885), i. 188.

commonplace reality that surrounded her, seemed to lay bare the
future too, and bring out into oppressive distinctness all the details
of a weary life to be lived from day to day. . . . (ch. xvi)

The clear light on the objects in a room, the definiteness and
dreariness, and the suggestion of a prosaic present stretching into
an unchanging prosaic future are the unmistakable links with the
first image in the letter and the many later repetitions.

With Hetty Sorrel in *Adam Bede* it is the second look at a very
new loss of enchantment which makes her feel "that dry-eyed
morning misery, which is worse than the first shock, because it has
the future in it as well as the present" (ch. xxxi) and so it is with
Adam, on whom George Eliot bestows her own image of the well-lit
charmless room:

> now that by the light of this new morning he was come back to his
> home, and surrounded by the familiar objects that seemed for ever
> robbed of their charm, the reality—the hard, inevitable reality—of
> his troubles pressed upon him with a new weight. (ch. xxxviii)

This also echoes faintly the desolation of his mother, Lisbeth
Bede, when after her husband's death "the bright afternoon's sun
shone dismally" in her kitchen.[2] But for Lisbeth this is no disenchantment marking or making growth while for Adam, as for
Janet, the hard impact of reality is a crisis in nurture—he is far less
static than is often suggested. It is also a crisis which corresponds
to Hetty's and thus brings the two into oblique but organic relation.
His joyless vision of the world in which there is "no margin of
dreams beyond the daylight reality" recapitulates the common
unromantic daylight which drove her, ironically, to him. The
dreamless daylight makes the challenge which he accepts, propelled
as he is by the strong inseparable combination of his character and
his vocation, and which Hetty rejects in panic.

In "The Lifted Veil," the story published in *Blackwood's Magazine,* July 1859, the image of the lighted room recurs to stamp the
crisis, though the crisis is less one of disenchantment than one of

2. The light is transferred in metaphor to a second image of a ruined city.
This in its turn is an echo of a metaphor used to extend Janet's illumined
misery. Before it was shown in the unresponsive room it was compared with
"ruins lying blackened in the pitiless sunshine."

discovery. It is rather a melodramatic use of the image, partly because it is a metaphor and not the actual pressure of the seen
world, partly because of the feverish fantasy of the narrative:

> The terrible moment of complete illumination had come to me,
> and I saw that the darkness had hidden no landscape from me, but
> only a blank prosaic wall: from that evening forth, through the sicken-
> ing years which followed, I saw all round the narrow room of this
> woman's soul.

Here is the first appearance of the antithetical image of space
which in the later novels puts extra emphasis on the narrowness of
the room; but this is the only instance I know where the narrow
room is the woman's soul and not the soul's oppressive environment.

Maggie Tulliver's awakening from her dream, in *The Mill on the
Floss,* has enormous causal significance. It prepares her for her
second dream, made up of an unrealistic renunciation which is
both self-abnegation and self-indulgence, but it also prepares the
last and real awakening, when the revival of her old dream of
love and beauty in her meeting with Stephen leads first to the
drifting with the stream and then to the genuine renunciation.

The immediate causes of Maggie's disenchantment are the causes
of George Eliot's: family trouble, especially her father's illness, a
lasting feeling of separation, and sense of impotence and aspiration.
Here, although there is the emphasis of the dull and heavy prosaic
routine, we move away from the autobiographical images of light
and common objects:

> She could make dream-worlds of her own—but no dream-world
> would satisfy her now. She wanted some explanation of this hard,
> real life: the unhappy-looking father, seated at the dull breakfast
> table; the childish, bewildered mother; the little sordid tasks that
> filled the hours, or the more oppressive emptiness of weary, joyless
> leisure. (Bk. IV, ch. iii)

In *Romola* the images of light return, though not the common
objects. Romola's disenchanting illumination is something more
dramatic than the cold light of morning, as we might expect from
the novel which contains almost nothing of George Eliot's under-
statement of event and character. Romola loses her dream, the dream
of human fellowship and service, and she shrinks from "the light

of the stars, which seemed to her like the hard light of eyes that looked at her without seeing her" (ch. lxi). Like the common day-light in the other books the significance of the light is that it forces her to see the indifferent life outside the self.

Here too the image is repeated, and the repetition emphasizes a coincidence of character. Similar light falls on Savonarola, the parallel and the contrast to Romola. When he asks for a sign from Heaven there is a sudden stream of sunlight which lights his face and satisfies the crowd. But the effect is contemporary:

> when the Frate had disappeared, and the sunlight seemed no longer to have anything special in its illumination, but was spreading itself impartially over all things clean and unclean, there began, along with the general movement of the crowd, a confusion of voices. (ch. lxii)

Two chapters farther on the images of light are repeated. There is the light of common day in Savonarola's cell, contrasted with the colour and radiance of Fra Angelico's frescoes and especially his Madonna's "radiant glory":

> The light through the narrow windows looked in on nothing but bare walls, and the hard pallet and the crucifix.

This is the contrast (for the reader and not for the characters) between the glory and the hard reality. In the next chapter, Savonarola himself sees the light, the disenchanting light which is the image of the crowd's disillusion and which returns as the image of his own doubt:

> But there seemed no glory in the light that fell on him now, no smile of heaven: it was only that light which shines on, patiently and impartially, justifying or condemning by simply showing all things in the slow history of their ripening.

The images of light in *Romola* stand apart from those in the other books but they are still images of the light which shows a dreamless or unresponsive world outside the self.

In *Felix Holt* the description of brightly lit despair is put into the motto which prefaces chapter xliv:

> I'm sick at heart. The eye of day,
> The insistent summer noon, seems pitiless,

Shining in all the barren crevices
Of weary life, leaving no shade, no dark,
Where I may dream that hidden waters lie.

This fragment introduces Esther's endurance of the dream which comes true, in a different sense, "that state of disenchantment belonging to the actual presence of things which have long dwelt in the imagination with all the factitious charms of arbitrary arrangement" (ch. xliv). There is no place here for the dull and common room. Esther has to feel the oppression of spaciousness, of "a life of middling delights, overhung with the languorous haziness of motiveless ease, where poetry was only literature" (ch. xliv) and the light which shines too brilliantly for her is one she can put out: "she put out the wax lights that she might get rid of the oppressive urgency of walls and upholstery and that portrait smiling with deluded brightness" (ch. xlix). Once more the correspondences of character, the most significant thematic emphasis in the novels, are underlined by the common imagery. Part of Esther's disenchantment is the disenchanted face, in the portrait and outside, of Mrs. Transome, and Mrs. Transome's unbearable reality is also fixed in two images of light. There is the tragic desolation which is more violent than the awakening to prose reality:

> all around her, where there had once been brightness and warmth, there were white ashes, and the sunshine looked dreary as it fell on them. (ch. ix)

And there is the duller impact too, though again strengthened by metaphor:

> Here she moved to and fro amongst the rose-coloured satin of chairs and curtains . . . dull obscurity everywhere, except where the keen light fell on the narrow track of her own lot, wide only for a woman's anguish. (ch. xxxiv)

In the last novels we come back to the double image of light and common objects. Dorothea's disenchanted room, in *Middlemarch,* is of course the boudoir with the bow-window and the faded blue chairs. She comes back to it after her wedding journey to find a changed aspect:

The distant flat shrank in uniform whiteness and low-hanging uniformity of cloud. The very furniture in the room seemed to have shrunk since she saw it before: the stag in the tapestry looked more like a ghost in his ghostly blue-green world; the volumes of polite literature in the bookcase looked more like immovable imitations of books. The bright fire of dry oak-boughs burning on the dogs seemed an incongruous renewal of life and glow. (ch. xxviii)

The emphasis is on disenchantment—"Each remembered thing in the room was disenchanted, was deadened as an unlit transparency" —but the objects recede and grow small rather than strike the vision with their dullness or their hardness. And the light is not a brilliant one, either here or in the dazzling sunlight in a later scene in the same room where the real light is dulled in metaphor: "And just as clearly in the miserable light she saw her own and her husband's solitude—how they walked apart so that she was obliged to survey him." (ch. xlii)

When Gwendolen, in *Daniel Deronda,* meets an unmistakable impact from outside herself which breaks the steady dream of potential brilliance, she comes to realize the shock in a dull room. The image is almost a return to its origin:

the noonday only brought into more dreary clearness the absence of interest from her life. All memories, all objects, the pieces of music displayed, the open piano—the very reflection of herself in the glass—seemed no better than the packed-up shows of a departing fair. (ch. xxiii)

And, a little later:

But this general disenchantment with the world—nay, with herself, since it appeared that she was not made for easy pre-eminence—only intensified her sense of forlornness: it was a visibly sterile distance enclosing the dreary path at her feet. (ch. xxvi)

There is some interest in following the course of an image which suggested itself in experience or in imagination nine years before George Eliot began to write novels, and the persistent recurrence suggests both the impact of the first experience and the common thematic thread which runs from novel to novel. In order to look more clearly at the common element in these scenes of disenchantment—they are not the only examples but probably the most important—it is necessary to go back to the letter to Sara Hennell. After describing the awakening in the disenchanted room George Eliot writes this:

> It is so in all the stages of life: the poetry of girlhood goes—the poetry of love and marriage—the poetry of maternity—and at last the very poetry of duty forsakes us for a season, and we see ourselves, and all about us, as nothing more than miserable agglomerations of atoms—poor tentative efforts of the Natur Princep to mould a personality.[3]

This disappearance of glamour is an essential part of the process of every novel, and this letter is almost a forecast of what she was to write: the poetry of girlhood vanishes for Janet and Maggie, the poetry of love and marriage for Gilfil, Hetty, Adam, Silas, the poetry of maternity for Mrs. Transome, and the poetry of duty for Romola. Moreover, each conversion of poetry into prose depends on the dispelling of a dream. This poetry is usually not a lost glory, as it is in Wordsworth and Coleridge, and perhaps in Newman.[4] It is a poetry erected on a dream, a dream in which the dreamer occupies the centre, and disenchantment is the waking which forces the dreamer to look painfully at a reality which puts him in his place. Janet, Adam, Maggie, Esther, Romola, and Dorothea all move out of their different dreams into the same clearly lit world where they have to do without the dreamer's drug. The crisis is one of the oblique demonstrations of George Eliot's precept, enunciated as the positivist's challenge to Christianity: "The 'highest calling and election' is to *do without opium*." [5] George Eliot does not show her own renunciation of opiate, but she shows opiates as various as alcohol, daydream, literature, love, and inexperienced idealism. Most of her heroines need only one disenchantment, though Hetty and Gwendolen withdraw from their disenchanted worlds to find

---

3. Cross, op. cit., i. 189.
4. Newman is closest to George Eliot: "Alas! what are we doing all through life, both as a necessity and as a duty, but unlearning the world's poetry, and attaining to its prose!" *The Idea of a University*, Part II, ch. iv (1854-6), quoted by G. Tillotson in *Criticism and the Nineteenth Century* (London, 1951), p. 166.
5. Cross, op. cit., ii. 283.

some other temporary opiate. Their failure to find nurture in despair is as significant as the success of Dorothea.

"Nothing more than miserable agglomerations of atoms"—the sense of dislocation within the personality was something which George Eliot felt as strongly as Wordsworth and Coleridge had before her. Her metamorphosis, as she called it, was indeed like Wordsworth's in more ways than one. They were both haunted by a double sense of disintegration: by the break between past and present, and by the break between the heart and the reason.

It is the first break, the loss of continuity in time, the sense of an isolated present snapped off from the past, which she emphasizes most vigorously in the novels. In their very different ways Maggie, Silas, Esther, Dorothea, and Gwendolen all share with their creator this feeling of fragmentariness and unreality. In their lives, as in hers, it was a stage in the metamorphosis. For most of them the break with the past is a break with an opiate, with the exception of Silas, whose opiate was provided by the very isolation of the present. For him exile in place and hence in time was desirable:

> Minds that have been unhinged from their old faith and love, have perhaps sought this Lethean influence of exile, in which the past becomes dreamy because its symbols have all vanished, and the present too is dreamy because it is linked with no memories. (ch. ii)

George Eliot too had rejected the symbols of her past, and her fear of emotional isolation from the past and from her family is retold, with a difference, in the progress of Silas.

Silas is perhaps not strictly relevant to this discussion since he is one of the very few characters who is not absorbed in the dream of self. This is why his disintegration is a pleasantly unreal state, whereas most of the disenchanted heroines feel clearly and harshly aware of a reality which blocks past from present. It is a blocking which ends the dream of self, which marks the rude and salutary awakening to the world where self is reduced. Gwendolen's awakening stands alone in this respect for it is a slow process, not fairly simply identified with the awakening disenchantment which alters both past and present. Even in her disenchanted moment she is preoccupied with self, and she has to go far before her dread of solitude becomes an acceptance of solitude. Again, the process is given unity by the repeated images. Just as the dead face in the portrait makes the objective premonition of Grandcount's death, so the first image of space prepares us for the last. We are told that her fear of

> Solitude in any wide scene impressed her with an undefined feeling of immeasurable existence aloof from her, in the midst of which she was helplessly incapable of asserting herself. (ch. vi)

This is kept alive in faint echoes throughout the book until it is repeated and justified in the crisis of her parting with Deronda, where we see her

> for the first time being dislodged from her supremacy in her own world, and getting a sense that her horizon was but a dipping onward of an existence with which her own was revolving. (ch. lxix)

For Gwendolen, and for many of the others, disenchantment works, slowly or quickly, towards "the state of prostration—the self-abnegation through which the soul must go," as George Eliot described it in the letter to Sara Hennell quoted at the beginning. Gwendolen even shares with George Eliot the sense of physical shrinking. Gwendolen felt that she was reduced to a "speck"; George Eliot says in this same letter:

> I feel a sort of madness growing upon me—just the opposite of the delirium which makes people fancy that their bodies are filling the room. It seems to me as if I were shrinking into that mathematical abstraction, a point.[6]

In the feeling of self-annihilation George Eliot is closer to Keats than to Wordsworth or Coleridge.

Whether or not they are reduced to a point, her heroines are certainly forced from the centre to the periphery, from the dream of self which filled the world to a reduced consciousness. The place of the oppressive room in this process is plain. It is the physical enclosure, the daily life, the woman's place. For all the heroines the forcible reduction is in part at least the realization of the woman's lot, and the image of the room is the appropriate feminine image of the shut-in life. The hard reality of the common objects is the

6. Cross, op. cit., i. 189.

only furnishing for the social trap portrayed in *The Mill on the Floss, Middlemarch* (perhaps to a lesser extent), and *Daniel Deronda*.

Not that the image is only a plea for the imprisoned woman. It can present Adam Bede's despair of himself and his world, and indeed any crisis in the development of the egoist—and all her characters are egoists—in which self shrinks and vision expands. Three weeks after she wrote to Sara Hennell describing her disenchantment, she wrote, with a backward glance:

> All creatures about to moult, or to cast off an old skin, or enter on any new metamorphosis, have sickly feelings. It was so with me. But now I am set free from the irritating worn-out integument.[7]

This is the important thing. The disenchantment marks a stage in metamorphosis: it is the well-lit day which makes George Eliot's dark night of the soul. It is a test and a prelude to change. The idealists, Adam, Romola, and Dorothea, are forced to recognize the egoism in their ideal. The egoists who are successfully nurtured, Maggie and Esther, are forced to abdicate their splendid dreams. But classification is too rough a process. There is all the difference in the world between Maggie's reaction to disenchantment and Esther's: Maggie's prosaic shock leads her into a new dream of theoretical renunciation, Esther's leads her to accept as bitter what had been sweet in the dream. Maggie is roused by the twin shocks of sympathy and helplessness, Esther by the ironical solidifying of her romantic dream. There is also Hetty, caught in the "narrow circle of her imagination," able to do nothing but run desperately from the unbearable daylight. There is Gwendolen, who has to endure a triple disenchantment before she abandons the place of the princess. The pattern remains, the people change. To point to a common image which links character and theme is merely to point to a constant which throws all the variations into relief. George Eliot used the landmarks of her own way of the soul—and this may be one reason why she is sometimes said to use one heroine many times —but it is only the landmarks which are unchanging.

Even the landmarks change in details. The disenchanted objects change. Janet sees ordinary chairs and tables, as George Eliot did, but Adam sees the dressing-table he made for Hetty. Esther sees

7. Cross, op. cit., i. 190.

richer furniture, and Mrs. Transome's portrait, while Dorothea sees the tapestry she had welcomed because it belonged to Casaubon's mother, and, as the one living object, the portrait of Ladislaw's grandmother. Gwendolen, the aspiring amateur rebuked by Klesmer, the beauty whose face is her fatal fortune, sees the piano and the mirror.

What is more, for Esther and Dorothea and Gwendolen there is the movement away from the image of the narrow room. Gwendolen's sense of space has terror in it, but in its implications it is not so very different from the triumph in space which is found in *Felix Holt* and *Middlemarch*. Esther and Dorothea look away from the dead objects and see people: they look at a light which has some promise. Esther wanted "the largeness of the world to help her thought" (ch. xlix) and she turns from the room to the window. Dorothea does the same. She

> could see figures moving. . . . Far off in the bending sky was the pearly light; and she felt the largeness of the world and the manifold wakings of men to labour and endurance. (ch. lxxx)

What was a single image becomes a significant antithesis. The narrow room marks one stage in metamorphosis, the open window another.

George Eliot's Conception of "Form"

by Darrel Mansell, Jr.

George Eliot's late novels are very complex. They attempt to embrace a broad diversity of characters and events (the "panoramic view" she says she had tried to achieve in *Middlemarch*[1]); and it is not obvious what, if anything, she considers the unifying principle that should bring all the parts together into a unified whole. In a letter written in 1866 John Blackwood comments that *Felix Holt* is "not like a Novel"; it is, he thinks, a "series of panoramas" (*Letters*, IV.243). The reviewer of *Felix Holt* for the *Edinburgh Review* objects that the "story has the defect of running in two parallel lines with only an occasional and arbitrary connexion."[2] Henry James finds *Middlemarch* a "treasure-house of details, but . . . an indifferent whole."[3] And F. R. Leavis in *The Great Tradition* is willing to cut away the "bad part" of *Daniel Deronda* and allow the story of Gwendolen Harleth to stand by itself.[4]

Recent criticism has developed the idea that one unifying principle in *Middlemarch* is the principle of analogy: that Casaubon and Lydgate (as one instance), who have very little to do with each other in the plot, are related by the analogy that both are searching for a kind of "primitive tissue" (Casaubon's "Key to all Mythologies"; Lydgate's medical research).[5] Likewise, Rosamond Vincy and

---

"George Eliot's Conception of 'Form' " by Darrel Mansell, Jr. From *Studies in English Literature*, 5 (Autumn, 1965), 651–62. Copyright © 1965 by William Marsh Rice University. Reprinted by permission of *Studies in English Literature*.

1. *The George Eliot Letters*, ed. Gordon S. Haight, 7 vols. (London, 1954–1956), V.241. Hereafter cited as *Letters*.
2. "Felix Holt, the Radical," *Edinburgh Review*, CXXIV (1866), 444.
3. "Middlemarch," *Galaxy*, XV (1873), 425.
4. See *The Great Tradition* (Garden City: Doubleday, 1954), p. 150.
5. See David R. Carroll, "Unity Through Analogy: An Interpretation of *Middlemarch*," *Victorian Studies*, II (1959), 310–311.

Madame Laure, who have nothing whatever to do with each other in the plot, are related by the analogy that both are a kind of basil plant which flourishes on a murdered man's brains. (Madame Laure murders her husband for her own convenience; Rosamond forces Lydgate to give up his research and become a successful spa doctor.)[6]

There is more evidence than what can be gathered from the novels themselves that George Eliot intended analogies like these to be a unifying principle in her fiction. A most important piece of evidence has been overlooked: George Eliot has given a kind of theory of art, in her "Notes on Form in Art (1868)." These notes have received almost no attention in the vast criticism of her fiction during the past few years; yet they are the most important single source of information on what George Eliot was trying to do in her novels. As I shall try to show, they make clear how the principle of analogy is a unifying principle at work in her novels; they explain her conception of "form"; they reveal a reason why she does not consider the beginnings and endings of her novels as important as the "inner relations"; and they hint, I think, that at the end of her career she had pressed her conception of "form" so far that the beginnings and endings of her novels had become a source of frustration.

In these "Notes on Form in Art (1868)" George Eliot maintains that, when we consider any object (as an instance not given in the "Notes" we might consider a tree), we first consider the thing as a whole in itself. We then discriminate that the whole is composed of parts (the trunk and leaves); and that the whole is part of a larger whole (a meadow). It is our act of discriminating that the original whole is composed of parts, and that the original whole is itself a part of a larger whole, that, to George Eliot's mind, gives the tree "form" for us. The "form" of anything is our discrimination of "the relation of multiplex interdependent parts to a whole which is itself in the most varied & therefore the fullest relation to other wholes." [7] Form shows how something is related to its environment;

6. See Suzanne C. Ferguson, "Mme. Laure and Operative Irony in *Middle-march*: A Structural Analogy," *Studies in English Literature*, III (1963), 513.

7. Notebook, ca. 1865–1869 (Yale University Library), p. 2. The "Notes" begin in the back of the Notebook and proceed toward the front, Notebook inverted. The references are to George Eliot's page numbers. The Notebook is described

and if George Eliot wanted to give the form (as distinct from the "outline": see below) of a tree, she would feel bound to introduce the relations of the tree to the soil, of the soil to the grass, and so on. A visual description of what the tree looks like does not constitute its form; the form is rather the relation of the tree to its environment. Form is not outward appearance but "inward" relations.

She thinks the "highest Form" is "the most varied group of relations bound together in a wholeness which again has the most varied relations with all other phenomena" (p. 3). Taken strictly, such a conception of form frustrates her art: she could completely render the form of the tree only by giving all the relations of the tree to the rest of the universe, for everything is in some way related to everything else. Her universe is bound together by Carlyle's "organic filaments." For Carlyle there is not a "leaf rotting . . . but is indissoluble portion of solar and stellar systems . . .";[8] and for George Eliot in *Middlemarch* the universe is a "tempting range of relevancies" (II.xv; I.214).[9] She despairs of ever giving a complete account in her fiction of how any part of it is related to the rest. The "narrator of human action," if he did his work with completeness, "would have to thread the hidden pathways of feeling and thought which lead up to every moment of action . . ." (an extract from the motto, *Daniel Deronda*, II.xvi; I.244).

Because the "highest Form" is "the most varied group of relations bound together in a wholeness which again has the most varied relations with all other phenomena," she strives to make the "relations" in her fiction as complex as possible. But the kind of complexity George Eliot tries to achieve has nothing to do with the mere number of characters and incidents in her novels. The com-

---

by Bernard J. Paris, "George Eliot's Unpublished Poetry," *Studies in Philology*, LVI (1959), 539–558; and the "Notes" have been published in *Essays of George Eliot,* ed. Thomas Pinney (New York, 1963), pp. 431–436.

8. For "organic filaments" see *Sartor Resartus* (first English edition 1838), Book I, Chapter xi. George Eliot praises *Sartor Resartus* in a letter of 1841 (*Letters*, I.122–123). The quotation above appears in "The Hero as Poet," *On Heroes, Hero Worship* . . . (1841), in *The Works of Thomas Carlyle,* 30 vols. (London: Centenary Ed. [1899–1923?], V.102.

9. References are to the Cabinet Edition of George Eliot's works, 24 vols. (Edinburgh and London: William Blackwood, [1877–1885]). Volume and page numbers follow book and chapter.

plexity is rather the number of what she calls "relations" among what characters and incidents there are. In her "Quarry" for *Middlemarch* she has taken the trouble to enter under "Relations to be developed" a list of eleven, such as Bulstrode's to Raffles, and Ladislaw's to Mr. Brooke.[10] These "relations" give the novel its "form"; and she thinks that the more relations there are, the higher the form.

George Eliot enthusiastically reviewed Ruskin's *Modern Painters, III* (1856) for the *Westminster Review*; and earlier that year she had noted in a letter that she and Lewes "are delighting ourselves with Ruskin's 3d volume, which contains some of the finest writing I have read for a long time . . ." (*Letters*, II.228). Her idea in the "Notes" that the form of art becomes higher as the art exhibits more and more relations, of the kind she lists in the *Quarry*, follows Ruskin's principle in *Modern Painters, III* that the "great artist chooses the most necessary [truths] first, and afterwards the most consistent with these, so as to obtain the greatest possible . . . sum." [11] Both Ruskin and George Eliot have a way of actually totaling up the number of "truths" (for Ruskin), or "relations" (for George Eliot), in order to determine whether a given work is great or not. Great art does not move toward simplicity, but toward complexity. Ruskin would accept the proposition that, if all other things could be considered equal, a work of art exhibiting three truths consistent with the most necessary ones would be greater than a work of art exhibiting two; and George Eliot would accept the proposition that a work of art in which the eleven relations she lists in the *Quarry* were bound together in a wholeness would exhibit a higher form than if only ten were bound together. There are degrees of form, and the higher the degree the better. George Eliot finds that as any art develops toward a higher degree of form it invariably bcomes more complex as the artist develops more "relations" within the form. Her notes "Versification (1869)" observe that "in every art that reaches a high degree of practice, the use of

10. *Quarry for Middlemarch*, ed. Anna Theresa Kitchel (Berkeley and Los Angeles, 1950), p. 45. The *Quarry* appears as a supplement to *Nineteenth-Century Fiction*, IV (1949–1950).

11. *Works*, ed. Cook and Wedderburn, 39 vols. (London: Library Edition, 1903–1912), V.59.

the medium discloses new & newer relations in that medium, so that the artist in his turn confers fresh associations. . . ." [12]

She finds that the most perfect example of "the most varied group of relations bound together in a wholeness which again has the most varied relations with all other phenomena" is an organism, the human body. The "highest Form," she points out in the "Notes on Form in Art (1868)," is the "highest organism" (p. 3); and in a letter she refers to the process by which each of her own novels becomes a "complete organism" (*Letters*, V.324). In her letters she commonly uses organic metaphors to describe how her stories "grow" in her like plants, "unfold" themselves. But it is not merely the complexity of the human organism which makes it the highest form; it is the fact that the complex relations are bound together in a wholeness. In an organism, as opposed, for instance, to a rock, there is a "consensus or constant interchange of effects among its parts" ("Notes," p. 5). The word "consensus" to her "expresses that fact in a complex organism by which no part can suffer increase or diminution without a participation of all other parts . . . & a consequent modification of the organism as a whole" (p. 5). This "consensus" that makes it impossible to disturb any part of a complex organism without upsetting the whole may follow Ruskin's "Sincerity" in *Modern Painters, III,* which term George Eliot in her review paraphrases as "the largest possible quantity of truth in the most perfect possible harmony." [13]

George Eliot considers that her novels are bound together in such a "consensus" or harmony. In defending herself against "preaching" she declares in a letter that "if I have ever allowed myself in dissertation or in dialogue [anything] which is not part of the *structure* of my books, I have there sinned against my own laws" (*Letters*, V.459). She is more anxious, I think, than most Victorian novelists that her novels be considered as organic wholes. She refused at one point to tell John Blackwood the remainder of the "story" of *Adam Bede* "on the ground that I would not have it judged apart from my *treatment*" (*Letters*, II.503–504); and in a letter discussing *Daniel Deronda* she objects to the "laudation of

12. Notebook, ca. 1865–1869 (Yale), George Eliot's p. 9.
13. "Art and Belles Lettres," *Westminster Review,* LXV (1856), 628; see Ruskin's *Works,* V.58 ff.

readers who cut the book into scraps. . . . I meant everything in the book to be related to everything else there" (*Letters*, VI.290). If the form of the novel is "organic," there is a "consensus" or harmony of the parts that prevents excising any part without damaging the entire organism. In the "Notes" she makes a distinction between the "accidental" form of a rock, which allows the rock to be split without altering the composition of either half, and the form of an organism, which prevents the organism from being divided without altering the whole composition (pp. 4–5); and to Professor Leavis's suggestion that the part of *Daniel Deronda* concerned with Daniel Deronda could be cut away from the part concerned with Gwendolen Harleth, she might have replied that, if the novel has achieved an organic form, it is no more possible to divide Deronda from Gwendolen than to divide Gwendolen herself.

Only the human organism, George Eliot points out in the "Notes," "comprises things as diverse as the fingernails & toothache, as the nervous stimulus of muscle manifested in a shout, & the discernment of a red spot on a field of snow; but all its different elements . . . are bound together in a more necessary wholeness . . . than can be found in any other existence known to us" (pp. 2–3). In striving for the highest possible form in her novels, she tries to bring together into a "wholeness" characters and events of the most diverse possible "relations." In letters she mentions the *"epische Breite"* of *The Mill on the Floss,* and the "panoramic view" she had tried to achieve in *Middlemarch* (*Letters*, III.317; see also III.362; V.241). The more varied relations she can present in her fiction, the higher the degree of form she can attain if she is successful in binding everything together in a wholeness.

She presses the reader to find relationships among the most seemingly disconnected events. Even in the early "The Sad Fortunes of the Rev. Amos Barton," for instance, the architectural history of Shepperton Church and the sad fortunes of its curate are brought into a relationship: it is when the old church is "half pulled down" (*Scenes of Clerical Life,* "Amos Barton," v; I.69) that his wife Milly falls ill; and the sentence revealing the completion of the new church (ix; I.118) is followed by the appearance of the letter from Carpe which forces Barton to resign. In "Mr. Gilfil's Love-Story," "while Cheverel Manor was growing from ugliness into beauty,

Caterina too was growing . . ." (iv; I.193). In *Silas Marner,* as
Eppie's "mind was growing into knowledge, [Silas's] mind was
growing into memory" (xiv; 193–194). In the first example the
significance of the relationship seems to be that Amos Barton, who is
"the quintessential extract of mediocrity" (v; I.73), cannot survive in
the world of "New-varnished efficiency" (i; I.4) which the new church
has been made to symbolize; in the second example the new Cheverel
Manor is built by Italian workmen brought from Italy by Sir
Christopher, just as he has brought Caterina; and in the third
(and most obvious) Silas's caring for Eppie's education has caused
him to remember his own tender past.

As George Eliot develops her art to a higher and higher degree
of form, the "relations" she tries to bind together in a wholeness
become much more diverse than these. The Proem of *Romola*
prepares the reader to find the "broad sameness of the human
lot" in what follows. By "broad sameness' she means more than that
"we still resemble the men of the past more than we differ from
them" (Proem; I.2); for in the novel itself characters who run
through their careers for the most part independent of one another
(as do Casaubon and Lydgate in *Middlemarch*) are shown to have
broadly the same lots. As Tito Melema, for instance, looks down on
Savonarola on the day of the Trial by Fire, George Eliot points
out the "common turning-point towards which those widely-
sundered lives had been converging" (III.lxv; II.371); and it is on
the day Tito dies that Savonarola is tortured into confessing (see
III.lxviii; II.395). Likewise, Romola and Savonarola run through
their careers for the most part independent of each other. Savonarola personally interferes in Romola's life only when he turns her
back to Florence (II.xl); and she personally interferes in his life only
when she pleads in vain for her godfather (III.lix). Yet George Eliot
emphasizes that the "problem before . . . [Romola] was essentially
the same as that which had lain before Savonarola—the problem
where the sacredness of obedience ended, and where the sacredness
of rebellion began" (III.lvi; II.273); and apparently with this
passage in mind she points out in a letter that the "great problem"
of Romola's life "essentially coincides with a chief problem in
Savonarola's" (*Letters,* IV.97). It is a rough index of how far George
Eliot reaches out after more and more diverse "relations" to bind

together in a wholeness that in *Romola* she makes the relation of
Romola and Savonarola explicit by a statement in the text; and in
Middlemarch the similar relations of Casaubon and Lydgate, and of
Rosamond and Madame Laure, have been the subject of articles
by critics.

Just as *Felix Holt*, which follows *Romola*, promises to show
the "mutual influence of dissimilar destinies (iii; I.73), so *Middlemarch*, which follows *Felix Holt*, calls the reader's attention to the
"stealthy convergence of human lots" (I.xi; I.142) that do not
appear to be related. Featherstone and Casaubon, for instance, who
have next to nothing to do with each other in the plot, both die
without having been able to deliver up their writings to the world
in a decisive form: Featherstone while clasping the key to the chest
containing his two wills (III.xxxiii); Casaubon after having "ex-
hausted himself" (V.xlviii; II.317) on a work that is still in note-
books. Ladislaw's refusal to accept money from Bulstrode when the
latter has been exposed (VI.lxi) is related to Caleb Garth's giving
up the management of Bulstrode's lands (VII.lxix), As David Carroll has noticed, Lydgate's attempt to find the "primitive tissue" is
related to Casaubon's Key to all Mythologies. Even Dorothea's marriage is obscurely related to Brooke's standing for Middlemarch in
the election; and the two events are confused by Sir James Chettam
and Mr. Cadwallader (see I.vi; I.viii).[14]

In *Middlemarch* George Eliot has come a long way from the more
or less obvious "relations" of Amos Barton and Shepperton Church.
In *Middlemarch* the reader is offered little help: he must establish
the relations as best he can. To repeat, the relation of Savonarola
and Romola is made explicit; the relation of Casaubon and Lydgate
is not. In her late fiction George Eliot moves from easy and explicit
relations to obscure implicit ones. The Introduction to *Felix Holt*
described the enchanted forest where there are thorn-bushes that
have human histories hidden in them (I.13); and the final words of
the Introduction, "These things are a parable," give the reader a

---

14. For Carroll's article, see note 5. The relation of Lydgate's project to
Casaubon's is further borne out in *Theophrastus Such* by the dilettante Merman,
who himself attempts two similar projects: the "ultimate reduction of all the
so-called elementary substances" (p. 48), and the "possible connection of certain
symbolic monuments common to widely scattered races" (p. 50).

clue that these things are related to the "secrets" (i; I.23) in the history of Mrs. Transome which follows. The Prelude to *Middlemarch* introduces Saint Theresa and "later-born Theresas" (I.2); but the Prelude concludes without any word of advice on how the Prelude is related to the story of Dorothea Brooke which follows. The relation of these two human lots develops stealthily in the novel, and the relation is confirmed only in the Finale, where the "many Theresas" of the Prelude become "many Dorotheas" (III.465).

In George Eliot's last novel, *Daniel Deronda*, the two human lots, Daniel Deronda's and Gwendolen Harleth's, run through the novel almost completely independent of each other (the two characters, for instance, exchange glances in the first scene, part, are not introduced to each other until Book IV, Chapter xxix, and at the conclusion have parted forever). The "occasional and arbitrary connexion" of two parallel plot lines which the early critic complained of in *Felix Holt* has been carried so far here that Professor Leavis could propose cutting one from the other. What makes the two a "wholeness" is the complex of analogical relations between them (for instance, both Deronda and Gwendolen are searching for a duty to submit to, which Deronda at last finds in his Jewish heritage, and which Gwendolen never finds). By so reducing the interrelations in the plot itself, George Eliot has pressed the principle of unity by analogy to an extreme; and has in a sense opened the way for James Joyce's *Ulysses*, in which Stephen Dedalus and Leopold Bloom run for the most part independent courses which generate between them the analogical relations (such as Stephen's search for a father, Bloom's for a son) that are the important meaning of the novel.

Indeed in *Middlemarch* and *Daniel Deronda* the "relations" among characters and events have become so diverse that the "wholeness" threatens to be George Eliot's private experience which the reader experiences only partially and tentatively. The diversity which her kind of form can include is limited only by what she herself thinks she is able to bind together in a wholeness in her own mind. What is structure, she asks in the "Notes," except a "set of relations selected & combined in accordance with the sequence of mental states in the constructor, or with the preconception of a whole which he has inwardly evolved?" (p. 3). She is apparently not at all concerned that if this definition of structure is pressed to the limit anything that comes into the author's mind as he writes can find a place in his fiction. For George Eliot the psychology of the author makes just as valid a relation between characters and events as the logic of time and place in the plot. She maintains in the "Notes" that the structure of fiction is determined by the "sequence of mental states" (p. 3) in the mind of the author; and not necessarily, for instance, by the sequence of the events the author is talking about. The reader, forced in this late fiction to make relations which rise, as it were, above what is happening in the plot, is thrown upon his own ability to re-experience intellectual, thematic relationships which existed in the author's mind. He must see the "analogies" which David Carroll and Suzanne Ferguson discuss. He must see what Barbara Hardy calls "formal" relationships[15] among characters who have never met.

George Eliot's idea that form is "the most varied group of relations bound together in a wholeness which again has the most varied relations with all other phenomena" causes her to emphasize the multiplicity of "relations" within the novel, and to play down the novel's beginning and conclusion. These for her are not especially important. In the "Notes" she attempts to make a distinction between "form" and "outline." Outline is a "derivative meaning" of form, and is the "limit of that difference by which we discriminate one object from another . . ." (p. 4). She means that the "outline" of something is its visual appearance (earlier, p. 3, she couples "outline & visual appearance"): the "line" for instance, "with which a rock cuts the sky" (p. 5). Outline is "determined partly by the intrinsic relations or composition of the object, & partly by the extrinsic action of other bodies upon it" (p. 4). In the case of an inorganic body, the outline is determined by a nearly equal struggle between these two forces; but in the case of an organic body the outline is determined almost entirely by the intrinsic relations. Thus, extending the examples that appear in the notes, the outline of a rock is determined by a nearly equal struggle between the attrition of wind and rain on the rock, and the intrinsic hardness of the rock; whereas the outline of a man is determined almost entirely by the intrinsic relations of muscle to bone, and so on.

15. *The Novels of George Eliot* (London, 1959), p. 4.

The force of this distinction between how the outlines of inorganic and organic bodies are determined is to minimize the attention which the artist needs to give to the outline of an organic work of art. In an organic work the outline is determined almost entirely by the relations within (cf. Shelley's statement in *A Defense of Poetry* that poetry is a sword "which consumes the scabbard that would contain it"); and George Eliot expects the artist to concentrate his attention on the intrinsic relations. The outline, she maintains in the "Notes," will come from within, like a seashell (p. 6).

In the notes she does not make plain what the outline of a work of fiction would be; but by applying to a novel her general remark that outline is the "limit of that difference by which we discriminate one object from another . . ." (p. 4) it is of course obvious that the outline of a novel is the beginning and ending. Throughout her career she discourages the reader from giving as much significance to the beginning and ending as to the intrinsic relations of which these are only the outer limits. The first words of the first chapter motto of *Daniel Deronda* tell the reader that the poet can do nothing "without the make-believe of a beginning." She makes the point in a letter that "endings are inevitably the least satisfactory part of any work in which there is any merit of development" (*Letters,* VI.241–242). She speaks in a review of the "artificial necessities of a denouement." [16] And she maintains that "conclusions are the weak point of most authors, but some of the fault lies in the very nature of a conclusion, which is at best a negation" (*Letters,* II.324). Arthur Donnithorne's hellbent last-minute appearance with Hetty Sorrel's release, and the last-chapter flood that drowns Maggie Tulliver are, as it were, the negation of form by outline, the tree lopped and pruned into an artificial outline for reasons of necessity. We are not to scrutinize this outline, but the inner relations which constitute the form.

However this may be in theory (and there are serious objections to it), it does not in practice distract any reader from considering the conclusions of George Eliot's novels. The consensus is that they are her weak point. Ruskin, among many others, objects that she always makes her novels "end so wretchedly that they're worse than

16. "Art and Belles Lettres," *Westminster Review,* LXV (1856), 639.

none. . . ." Henry James knows "few things more irritating in a literary way than each of her final chapters. . . ." and Jerome Thale, in *The Novels of George Eliot,* observes that the "ending of a novel . . . was for George Eliot . . . a stumbling block." [17] But if her conception of form does not justify the endings, it indicates that to her they are not so important as the inner relations that give the novel form. If there has been any "merit of development" of these relations, the ending will not be satisfactory; there is a fault "in the very nature of a conclusion, which is at best a negation."

It is George Eliot's sense that there can be no satisfactory ending to a novel which exhibits this kind of form that seems to have frustrated her at the end of her career. For her concepton of form is in the end self-defeating. To the extent that she is able in her last novels to achieve a high degree of form by showing very intricate inner relations within a novel, the beginning and ending become increasingly false in that they artificially cut off relations which the novel itself sends outward, as it were, from its complexity to the rest of the universe. The more relations the novel establishes, the more must be severed where they do not end. When George Eliot says that the fault of a conclusion is that it is at best a "negation," she means that the form of the novel has shown "the most varied group of relations bound together in a wholeness which again has the most varied relations with all other phenomena"; and that at best the conclusion can only cut off this network at some arbitrary point. Thus "the artificial necessities of a denouement." Form, which attempts to show as many as possible of the relations which connect everything in George Eliot's universe to everything else, must always be incomplete. And the higher the form, the more incomplete.

Form for George Eliot must end where it does not really end. Every novel is torn ragged from its real context. The universe is a "tempting range of relevancies." The Finale of *Middlemarch* is not a finale, and begins, "Every limit is a beginning as well as an ending"; and in her huge last novel, *Daniel Deronda,* she seems

---

17. *Fors Clavigera, Works,* ed. Cook and Wedderburn, XXVII.538; *Views and Reviews* (Boston, 1902), p. 37; *The Novels of George Eliot* (New York, 1959), p. 146.

to have felt bound to make some apology for the "artificial necessities" her conception of form has imposed on her. The motto to the first chapter (noted above) refers to the "make-believe of a beginning"; and the motto concludes, "No retrospect will take us to the true beginning; and whether our prologue be in heaven or on earth, it is but a fraction of that all-presupposing fact with which our story sets out."

George Eliot, Feuerbach, and the Question of Criticism

by U. C. Knoepflmacher

In his just and perceptive evaluation of recent trends in George Eliot scholarship (*VS*, V [1961–62], 344–346), George Levine points to "gaps" that have to be filled by future critics of George Eliot if the sudden reputation of her novels is not to suffer once again by an equally abrupt "counter-revolution." Mr. Levine's advice is well-taken, but it fails, I think, to take into account the major gap which exists in George Eliot criticism today. This criticism has been singularly one-sided. Critics have either concentrated on a close scrutiny of George Eliot's art by fastening their attention on "form" and thus ignored or failed to exploit the ideological purposes which shape the formal features of her novels; or, conversely, aware of George Eliot's centrality as a Victorian thinker, they have reconstructed her ideology in the light of Darwin, Huxley, Comte, Mill, Spencer, Lewes, Hennell, Strauss, or Feuerbach. The latter approach has recently yielded Mr. Levine's own study of determinism in George Eliot's novels[1] and Bernard J. Paris's study of her "Religion of Humanity," [2] both of which contain definitive treatments of subjects first suggested by Basil Willey.[3] And yet, betrayed into

"George Eliot, Feuerbach, and the Question of Criticism" by U. C. Knoepfl-macher. From *Victorian Studies*, VII, No. 3 (March, 1964), 306–9. Copyright © 1964 by *Victorian Studies*. Reprinted by permission of *Victorian Studies*.

1. "Determinism and Responsibility in the Works of George Eliot," *PMLA*, LXXVII (1962), 268–279.
2. "George Eliot's Religion of Humanity," *ELH*, XXIX (1962), 418–443.
3. "George Eliot: Hennell, Strauss and Feuerbach," *Nineteenth Century Studies* (New York, 1949), esp. pp. 227–236.

the very same self-consciousness that he deplores in the writings of
the critics of the "formalistic" school, Mr. Levine hints at the in-
completeness of his and Mr. Paris's own approaches when he admits
that his discussion tends to treat "George Eliot as a philosopher
rather than an artist" (p. 268).

George Eliot is of course both artist and philosopher, and not
until we learn to deal with her simultaneously in these two roles
will we be able to do full justice to her work. It is false to assume
that, as a recent student of *Middlemarch,* Neil Isaacs, asserts, two
separate "principles" govern her novels and that these two principles, the one artistic and the other intellectual, must somehow
remain irrevocably apart in any intelligent discussion of her fiction.[4]
George Eliot successfully transmuted ideas into the form and structure of her novels. Formalistic critics like Barbara Hardy, Reva
Stump, or W. J. Harvey would have been immensely aided in their
discussion of "form" if they had not excluded the ideas and beliefs
that shaped George Eliot's novels. Others, like Joan Bennett or
Gerald Bullett, have been unable to fuse their discussion of George
Eliot's religious and philosophical foundations with their insight
into her novels. But lest I be accused of furnishing only what J. S.
Mill called a "negative criticism," let me provide also a "positive"
instance of that synthesis which, again after the fashion of Mill or
other Victorian "reconcilers," I hold to be so necessary to span the
gap that exists at present in our fragmented criticism of George
Eliot.

I should like to go to *Adam Bede* and to Feuerbach's *Essence of
Christianity* for my example of the criticism that I think is needed
to reckon with a "philosophic" novelist like George Eliot. In her
hunt for "patterns," Miss Stump has observed the "religious
imagery" in *Adam Bede;* in his reconstruction of George Eliot's
"religion of humanity," Mr. Paris has correctly evaluated her dependence on Feuerbach. But only through a combination of the
methods employed by both of these scholars can we get at the full
meaning of the symbology used in *Adam Bede* and thus penetrate
George Eliot's artistic and "philosophic" intentions in her portrayal
of Adam's development. In 1854, two and a half years before she

4. "*Middlemarch:* Crescendo of Obligatory Drama," *Nineteenth Century
Fiction,* XVIII (1963), 21–34.

began to write fiction, George Eliot acknowledged an indebtedness she seldom granted to any author: "With the ideas of Feuerbach I everywhere agree." [5] I should like to concentrate on a very small area of this "agreement" by pointing out how in *Adam Bede* she adopted his unorthodox explication of the Christian sacraments.

In *The Essence of Christianity*, Feuerbach, intent on recovering the "true or anthropological essence" of his man-centered religion, insisted that all rituals were merely a semi-conscious expression of man's veneration for the forces of nature. Contrasting the sacraments of Baptism to the Lord's Supper, he expounded the "moral and intellectual" significance of water, bread, and wine, and unabashedly invited the reader to participate in the "essential" rites he claimed to have rediscovered:

> Water, as a universal element of life, reminds us of our origin from Nature, an origin which we have in common with plants and animals. In Baptism we bow to the power of a pure Nature-force; water is the element of natural equality and freedom, the mirror of the golden age. But we men are distinguished from the plants and animals, which together with inorganic kingdom we comprehend under the common name of Nature;—we are distinguished from Nature. Hence we must celebrate our distinction, our specific difference. The symbols of this our difference are bread and wine. Bread and wine are, as to their materials, products of Nature; as to their form, products of man. If in water we declare: Man can do nothing without Nature; by bread and wine we declare: Nature needs man, as man needs Nature. In water, human mental activity is nullified; in bread and wine it attains self-satisfaction. . . . Hence this sacrament is only for man matured into consciousness; while baptism is imparted to infants.

Feuerbach concluded his unorthodox homily with this final exhortation:

> Hunger and thirst destroy not only the physical but also the mental and moral powers of man; they rob him of his humanity—of understanding, of consciousness. Oh! if thou shouldst ever experience such want, how wouldst thou bless and praise the natural qualities of bread and wine, which restore to thee thy humanity, thy intellect! It needs only that the ordinary course of things be interrupted in

5. *The George Eliot Letters*, ed. Gordon Haight (New Haven, 1954), II, 153.

order to vindicate to common things as uncommon significance, *to life,
as such, a religious import.* Therefore let bread be sacred for us, let
wine be sacred, and also let water be sacred! Amen.[6]

In *Adam Bede,* I suggest, George Eliot depicts the "mental and
moral" education of her protagonist through a series of symbolic
suppers which ultimately lead to his conversion to a Feuerbachian
"religion of suffering." The first of these suppers is designed to
remind Adam of his "origin of Nature," an origin represented by
Feuerbach through the symbol of water. The second scene, as
ironical as the first, stresses Adam's inability to see that man must
also be "distinguished from nature," a need soon to be accentuated
by Hetty's unnatural murder of her natural child. In the third
scene, Adam finally learns how to celebrate this "distinction" in a
manner which will give a truly "religious import" to life. This
scene, the most important of the three, relies entirely on Feuerbach's
allegorization of the Lord's Supper.

In the first supper-scene, the self-righteous Adam finishes a coffin
that his father has failed to deliver. He refuses to eat the food that
his mother proffers to him, but patronizingly allows his hungry
dog to devour his. Soon, however, he calls for "light and a draught
of water (beer was a thing only to be drunk on holidays)," accepts
a second "drop of water," and admits that he is getting "very
thirsty." [7] Adam works on, unaware that the intoxicated father to
whom he feels so superior has died a "watery death" in a nearby
creek (p. 50). His own tentative acceptance of the two sips of water
foreshadows his acceptance of his father's drunkenness when, later,
he discovers Thias's body, and a "flood of relenting and pity" sets
in and dissolves his hardness (p. 52). The symbol of water, like the
parallel between man and dog (an analogy repeatedly made by
Lisbeth, Dinah, Bartle Massey, Mrs. Poyser, and George Eliot herself), is designed to remind Adam of his subservience to and origin
from Nature, "an origin which we have in common with plants and
animals." For the water which has "nullified" the "mental activity"
of Adam's father, like "Gyp's mental conflict" between a rigid
"duty" and the instinctual "pleasure" of a meal (p. 40), stresses

6. Translated by George Eliot (Harper Torchbooks, 1957), pp. 275-278.
7. (Rinehart Edition, 1948), pp. 41, 45.

man's own integral part in the dual cycle of extinction and preservation which governs life. "Nature, that great tragic dramatist, knits us together by bone and muscle" (p. 37).

But if man, according to George Eliot and Feuerbach, must "bow" to the force of Nature, he must also know how to rise above it. Adam's ignorance of this second rule manifests itself at the supper which takes place during the young Squire's birthday feast. Sundered once again from his kin, Adam sits "upstairs" at the Squire's table, no longer drinking water, but the rich Loamshire ale. Somewhat pompously, he accepts a toast in which Arthur Donnithorne, the seducer of Adam's bride, wishes him to have "sons as faithful and clever as himself" (p. 274). The irony is obvious. Proud of his new capacity as keeper of the woods, Adam must still learn that his full "humanity" can only be celebrated through his "distinction" from Nature. Arthur and Hetty, the "natural" creatures he surprises in the woods he keeps, force upon him that suffering which, to George Eliot as to Feuerbach, can elevate man above the merely organic. For Hetty's "naturalness" is as deceptive as the beauty of "our English Loamshire," a landscape which lacks the images of the cross found in "foreign countries" as a visual reminder that "man's religion" cannot be merely a worship of impersonal forces: "No wonder man's religion has so much sorrow in it: no wonder he needs a Suffering God" (p. 371).

The third and most significant supper in this symbolic sequence marks the attainment of Adam's matured "consciousness." Sitting "upstairs" once again, but now in a bleak lodging in Stoniton, Adam has become "powerless to contemplate [the] irremediable evil and suffering" that surround Hetty's trial (p. 435). Unshaven, brooding, half-starved, he resembles David mourning the ugly beauty of Absalom. At this point, Bartle Massey the crippled schoolmaster, enters the room. Bartle tells Adam about the trial he has witnessed, while pressing on him "a bit of the loaf and some of that wine Mr. Irwine sent" (p. 437). But Adam pushes the cup aside. It is not until Bartle describes the pain of Hetty's uncle that Adam is willing to drink "a little" (p. 438). He asks about Hetty herself, and, on hearing about her suffering and the Rector's gentle actions, he is provoked into an exclamation: "God bless him, and you too, Mr. Massey" (p. 438). The involuntary blessing reverses his earlier exclamation about Hetty: "God bless her for loving me" (p. 374). For Adam can now signify his "distinction" from Nature in an act which George Eliot, resorting to an explication quite similar to Feuerbach's own, describes as "a baptism, a regeneration, the initiation into a new state" (p. 436). Adam promises to "stand by" Hetty at court. Immediately, the schoolmaster asks him to eat a "bit" and to drink "another sup, Adam, for the love of me" (p. 440). "Nerved by an active resolution, Adam took a morsel of bread, and drank some wine. He was haggard and unshaven, as he had been yesterday, but he stood upright again, and looked like the Adam Bede of former days" (p. 440).

Adam's conversion to that "new awe and new pity" that lie at the core of George Eliot's and Feuerbach's religions of humanity is thus completed. It seems hardly necessary to elaborate the symbolic parallel of this third supper taken by a "new" Adam, the bearded son of a carpenter, who "stood upright again." In an era in which we teach our students to hunt for "Christ-figures" in the works of Hemingway or Faulkner, such a parallel is all-too evident. But a "Christ-figure" is not simply an isolated "technique" or formalistic device. Adam's final transformation from communicant to humanist saviour is dependent on the author's deliberate purpose, a purpose which can be easily overlooked in a sheer examination of "patterns" or "movements." For the "movement" of the sequence I have traced is derived from Feuerbach's conclusion to his book: "Bread and wine typify to us the truth that Man is the true God and Saviour of man" (p. 277). There is of course a fourth supper-scene in *Adam Bede,* the Harvest Festival, but I believe that my point is made without further explication of the novel. If I have belabored this point, it is because I am convinced that only by treating George Eliot as a "philosophic" novelist can we do full justice to both her art and thought. George Eliot's Victorian readers understood this; even Henry James, after all a "Derondist of Derondists," merely suggested that her transmutation of philosophy into art was not as smooth as he would have liked it to be.

Mr. Levine is correct of course when he disparages the apologies, implicit or explicit, which have crept into practically all the one-sided discussions of George Eliot that we possess. To apologize for the nature of her art is not only futile, but also unfair. Mr. Levine, who, I know, would hardly like to see George Eliot dethroned in the "counter-revolution" he intimidates us with, seems, by these very fears, to be a doubter himself. I, for one, am more sanguine. George Eliot's present eminence has been attained without the cohesive approach her novels require, an approach combining the methods of the "new criticism" with those of the "history of ideas." I suspect, therefore, that our present high regard for George Eliot will only be confirmed and documented when the approach I have suggested is applied to the whole of her fiction.

An Interpretation of *Adam Bede*

by George R. Creeger

I

The virtual world created in *Adam Bede* possesses two major
divisions: the counties of Loamshire and Stonyshire (with their
villages, Hayslope and Snowfield).[1] The fact that they are not
merely literal recreations of Staffordshire and Derbyshire and that
the two places stand in complete antithesis is suggested by their
quasi-symbolic names.

Most of the action of the novel takes place in Loamshire, in and
around the village of Hayslope. Regarded together, the midland
shire and village constitute a kind of later-day Eden—a land of
Goshen,[2] at the very least. Protected on the north from "keen and
hungry winds" (I, 22) by the gentle heights of the Binton Hills,
Loamshire is a sheltered and fertile land, a "region of corn and
grass" (I, 22), where the farms (excepting those of such miscreants
as Luke Britton) produce the necessities and, indeed, the luxuries
of life in great abundance. Prosperity, if not omnipresent, is nevertheless common; poverty is rare. Exile from this snug world is re-

"An Interpretation of *Adam Bede*" by George R. Creeger. From *English
Literary History*, XXIII, No. 3 (September, 1956), 218–38. Copyright © 1956
by The Johns Hopkins Press. Reprinted by permission of The Johns Hopkins
Press.

1. The county seat of Stonyshire is called Stoniton. The other places named in
the novel (not belonging to the symbolic pattern set up in the Loamshire-Stony-
shire antithesis) are thinly disguised versions of real place names in Staffordshire
and Derbyshire.

2. *Adam Bede*, 2 vols., *The Works of George Eliot*, Cabinet Edition (Edinburgh [n.d.]), I, 50 (hereafter, and usually within the text, I shall give only the
volume number and page).

garded by its inhabitants as the worst evil that can befall them.[3]

Throughout the novel, however, we are reminded of a different sort of country—Stonyshire, where the land, naked under the sky, is barren and " 'where the trees are few, so that a child might count them, and there's very hard living for the poor in the winter' " (I, 48). The people of Stonyshire earn their livelihood not by tilling a fertile soil but by digging deep beneath the earth's surface in rocky mines or by laboring in the dark mills of sooty cities like Stoniton. In this " 'dreary bleak place' " (I, 129), poverty is the common lot of the people (I, 165).

At first glance Loamshire and Stonyshire seem like little more than a Victorian variation on the Romantic theme of country vs. city. It soon becomes apparent, however, that George Eliot has done more than simply broaden the negative symbol of the city (Stoniton) to include a surrounding wasteland (Stonyshire); she has handled the symbols in such a fashion that an inversion of their conventional values very nearly takes place. At least both Loamshire and Stonyshire are so stringently qualified that it is impossible to say of one that it is a positive, of the other a negative symbol. We discover that there is an ugly aspect to the green and fertile Loamshire world; and that despite the barrenness and sterility of Stonyshire, it is not altogether a wasteland.

The ways in which George Eliot goes about defining the symbolic relationship are occasionally clumsy, particularly for modern literary sensibilities with their strict demand that an author never intrude into his work. Like many another innocent Victorian, however, George Eliot does not hesitate to step in and speak directly to the point, telling us discursively, almost didactically, what Loamshire and Stonyshire represent. Only now and then does she trust the really very powerful imagery associated with the two worlds to carry alone the weight of definition. More usually she compromises by creating a dramatic situation in which conversations of characters about Loamshire and Stonyshire have a defining function, while she herself keeps discreetly in the background.

For example, much of Dinah Morris's function in the first part of

3. For example, it is clearly so regarded by Mrs. Bede (I, 57–58, 62–63, 178–179). The threat of exile is even more terrible for the Poysers (see I, 115; II, 91, 108, 155, 190–191, 265, 270–277).

the book is best understood in terms of a surrogate definer. Herself
a representative of the Stonyshire world, she nevertheless has family
attachments to Loamshire, where her aunt and uncle manage a
prosperous farm. Her position is ambiguous: because of her kinship
to the Poysers she commands a certain respect; at the same time
the community is essentially distrustful of her, both as an outsider
and as a Methodist.[4] Thus, when Dinah goes to the village green in
Hayslope to preach, every "generation . . . from old 'Feyther Taft'
. . . down to the babies" (I, 23) is near at hand, but "all took care
not to join the Methodists on the Green, and identify themselves
in that way with the expectant audience, for there was not one of
them that would not have disclaimed the imputation of having
come out to hear the 'preacher-woman,'—they had only come out
to see 'what war a-goin' on, like' " (I, 24).

Yet the sermon itself, as distinct from the act of a young un-
married woman's preaching on the green, scarcely touches the
villagers: if it is true that a hoyden named Chad's Bess is driven
by momentary fear of God's wrath to tear off the gaudy ear-bobs
she wears, it is equally true that for most of the villagers "a little
smouldering vague anxiety, that might easily die out again, was the
utmost effect Dinah's preaching had wrought" (I, 38). Dinah speaks
eloquently, both in prayer and sermon, of the evil in men's lives,
of the misery consequent upon sin and self-indulgence, and finally
of the possibility of redemption through love which turns all things
to good (I, 31–44). She has effectively stated the position of the
heart, yet what she has to say is largely ignored, or worse, received
apathetically. To Mr. Irwine, Rector of Hayslope, she later com-
plains:

> "But I've noticed, that in these villages where the people lead a
> quiet life among the green pastures and the still waters, tilling the
> ground and tending the cattle, there's a strange deadness to the
> Word, as different as can be from the great towns. . . . It's wonder-
> ful how rich is the harvest of souls up those high-walled streets,
> where you seemed to walk as in a prison-yard, and the ear is
> deafened with the sounds of worldly toil. I think maybe it is be-

4. Cf. the exchange between another stranger (Colonel Townley) and Casson,
the Hayslope innkeeper (I, 19); see also I, 287–288, and Claude T. Bissell, "Social
Analysis in the Novels of George Eliot," *ELH*, XVIII (September 1951), 230.

cause the promise is sweeter when this life is so dark and weary, and the soul gets more hungry when the body is ill at ease" (I, 134–135).

To Dinah's talk Mr. Irwine is a sympathetic listener. Not so Mrs. Poyser. Goaded almost beyond endurance when Dinah expresses surprise that Irwine had proved to be no " 'worldly Sadducee,' " she makes a characteristically sharp reply:

> "Pleasant! and what else did y' expect to find him but pleasant? . . . It's summat-like to see such a man as that i' the desk of a Sunday! As I say to Poyser, it's like looking at a full crop o' wheat, or a pasture with a fine dairy o' cows in it; it makes you think the world's comfortable-like. But as for such creaturs as you Methodisses run after, I'd as soon go to look at a lot o' bare-ribbed runts on a common. Fine folks they are to tell you what's right, as look as if they'd never tasted nothing better than bacon-sword and sour-cake i' their lives" (I, 137–138).

When Dinah suggests that there is something about the richness of Loamshire life that frightens her, Mrs. Poyser can only throw up her hands in uncomprehending disgust: " 'It passes my cunning to know what you mean by ease and luxury. . . . It's true there's good victual enough about you, as nobody shall ever say I don't provide enough and to spare; but if there's ever a bit o' odds an' ends as nobody else 'ud eat, you're sure to pick it out." [5]

The Bedes, equally representative of Loamshire, are equally at a loss (except for Seth) to understand Dinah's point of view: Mrs. Bede urges Dinah never to go back to Stonyshire, saying that her own husband, who had been born there, was in the right to leave it; so treeless a country would have been a poor place for a carpenter (I, 177). Adam expresses perfect contentment with Loamshire, calling Stonyshire a " 'hungry land' " (II, 158) and the village of Snowfield—"grim, stony, and unsheltered" (II, 158)—fellow to the country. Only Seth, himself a Methodist, and like Dinah clearly an exponent of the heart,[6] sympathizes with her love for the hill country.

5. II, 286; see the entire chapter, XLIX ("At the Hall Farm"), II, 281–294.
6. Seth stands in the sharpest possible contrast with Adam: where the latter is "keen," he is "mild" (see I, 5, 61, 64, 173), and is in this respect like both Dinah and his father (see I, 75).

In answer to these Loamshire dwellers, Dinah can only repeat what she has already said to her aunt: that there is something disquieting about the plenty of the land and that it would be difficult for her ever to turn her face toward a rich country, knowing that she was turning her back on a poor one, where people have a hard life " 'and the men spend their days in the mines away from the sunlight' " (I, 178). In Stonyshire at least the love of God is precious, and it is a blessing to carry the message of His love " 'to the lonely, bare, stone houses, where there's nothing else to give comfort' " (I, 178). To all of which Lisbeth says: " 'that's very well for ye to talk, as looks welly like the snowdrop-flowers as ha' lived for days an' days when I'n gethered 'em, wi' nothin' but a drop o' water an' a peep o' daylight; but th' hungry foulks had better leave th' hungry country' " (I, 178).

Obviously George Eliot is using Dinah, Mrs. Poyser, and the Bedes as a means of defining the symbolic relationship of Loamshire and Stonyshire: hearing about the two counties from Dinah, we sense a hardness lurking at the core of Loamshire which is spiritually stultifying. Yet the position taken by Mrs. Poyser and the Bedes is not without merit: they are saying, although each differently, that people who have known only a kind of attenuated existence are in no position to judge what life is, or should be. At the same time they fail to realize that hunger may be spiritual as well as physical. In these terms Loamshire is a hungry land, because some (at least) of its people, never having known privation and suffering, cannot therefore understand or sympathize with want, poverty, or even ugliness.[7] Like Loamshire itself such people may present to the world a beautiful, polished, or vital exterior, which nevertheless conceals a hardness at the core. Chief among such characters in the book are Mrs. Irwine (mother of the rector), Squire Donnithorne, and Martin Poyser.

Mrs. Irwine is a woman who judges by externals only: " 'Nature never makes a ferret in the shape of a mastiff. You'll never persuade me that I can't tell what men are by their outsides.' "[8] That she feels this way is partly the result of her own egotism: she is herself

7. See in particular II, 136.
8. I, 93; see also I, 228.

a very splendid old lady. Intelligent and penetrating, she has a
"small intense black eye," so "keen[9] and sarcastic in its expression"
that she looks at times almost like a gypsy fortune teller (I, 79).
Judging others by their appearance, she is careful of her own,
taking "a long time to dress in the morning." [10] Of her son she is
inordinately fond, even when she finds him on occasion too easy
tempered (I, 91). For her daughters, however, she cares less—is, in
fact, almost indifferent to them: they are plain and sickly, and
"splendid old ladies . . . have often slight sympathy with sickly
daughters" (I, 80).

Very much like Mrs. Irwine is old Squire Donnithorne. He too
is outwardly a splendid person, careful in his dress, icily polite in
his manners. "He was always polite," George Eliot writes, "but the
farmers had found out, after long puzzling, that this polish was one
of the signs of hardness. It was observed that he gave his most
elaborate civility to Mrs Poyser . . . inquiring particularly about
her health . . . Mrs Poyser curtsied and thanked him with great
self-command, but when he had passed on, she whispered to her
husband, 'I'll lay my life he's brewin' some nasty turn against us.
Old Harry doesna wag his tail so for nothin' " (I, 427–428).

As Mrs. Irwine represents the hardness of one level of the Loamshire world and the Squire another, so Mr. Poyser represents yet a
third, and quite possibly the most important: that of Mrs. Irwine
and Squire Donnithorne lies on the genteel fringes of the novel,
where it might be expected; Martin Poyser's hardness, however, lies
at the book's vital center. Almost an exact duplicate of the prosperous world in which he lives, he gives no external evidence of
hardness: well-fed, good-natured, he is an excellent husband and
loving father. But occasionally there are signs of severity in him,
as for example his attitude toward a neighbor, Luke Britton, whose
farm, like one described in *Walden,* is a "great grease-spot, redolent
of manures and buttermilk." Toward Britton he is absolutely un-
bending, "as hard and implacable as the north-east wind" (I, 214).
The reason is that the slovenly farmer violates all the principles
of good husbandry which Martin holds dear and which constitute

9. See also I, 255.
10. I, 80; see also I, 79.

a major part of his moral code, ranking second only to family honor. In a sense, therefore, we should be prepared for the complete lack of sympathy Martin exhibits toward Hetty when she too violates his moral code by bringing disgrace upon the family. Then, as the paterfamilias (but also clearly as representative of Loamshire) he is swift and unrelenting in his judgment of her (II, 189–190). Yet his severity takes us by surprise, much as it does Mrs. Poyser herself, who for once stands silent and in awe of her husband (II, 190).

These three characters, then, evidently stand in need of Dinah's message of sympathy and compassion. It would do them all good to live in Stonyshire for a while, to experience suffering and thereby add to the dimension of the head that of the heart—to become, in short, full human beings. This does not mean to become like Dinah. She is no more a complete personality at the beginning of the book than Hetty, for Dinah is all heart and passive receptivity; she lacks head. It does mean, however, to become like Mr. Irwine, Bartle Massey, and Mrs. Poyser, all (significantly enough) Loamshire dwellers, but separated from their compatriots because, unlike them, each has known some form of suffering or privation and is therefore able, in George Eliot's terms, to sympathize with the misery of others.

Bartle Massey, whose past is a mystery, is lame (I, 356). Mrs. Poyser, though sound of limb, has been in precarious health since the birth of her youngest child, Totty (I, 144–145). And if Mr. Irwine does not appear to have suffered very much himself, he has nevertheless known a good deal of vicarious misery, for both of his sisters are sickly and one, with whom he is invariably sympathetic, suffers from stunning migraines. Furthermore, he has had to forego marriage in order, ironically enough, to support in style a mother whose hardness toward her daughters is a source of constant distress to him (I, 98).

Because of their knowledge of suffering these characters are compassionate: they possess the attributes of heart as well as head; their worldly knowledge and keen intelligence are always tempered by sympathy and love. This balance of head and heart is usually presented dramatically through characters' actions; we also hear of it directly from the author when, in speaking of someone like Mrs.

Poyser, she repeatedly links the words "keenness" and "mildness" (or equivalents).

In the case of Mrs. Poyser we are perhaps inclined to remember only that she is keen,[11] agreeing with Mr. Irwine that " 'her tongue is like a new-set razor' " (II, 93), or recalling the "freezing arctic ray" (I, 107) of her glance. But there is another dimension to her personality which we are never permitted to forget. From Adam, for example, we learn that if " 'her tongue's keen, her heart's tender' " (II, 361). It is as mother to the ever-naughty Totty that this combination of mildness and keenness, head and heart, is made most clear: the sight of her child riding secure on Adam's shoulders is pleasant to her: " 'Bless your sweet face, my pet,' she said, the mother's strong love filling her keen eyes with mildness." [12]

The same combination of keenness and mildness is characteristic of Mr. Irwine too. We read that "there was a certain virtue in that benignant yet keen countenance, as there is in all human faces from which a generous soul beams out" (I, 297). What is true of Irwine is equally true of Bartle Massey. As a teacher he is wrathful with erring youth; but with those mature men, common laborers, who come to him that they may learn to read, he is all patience and mildness; for them his face

> wore its mildest expression: the grizzled bushy eyebrows had taken their more acute angle of compassionate kindness, and the mouth, habitually compressed with a pout of the lower lip, was relaxed so as to be ready to speak a helpful word or syllable in a moment. This gentle expression was the more interesting because the school-master's nose, an irregular aquiline twisted a little on one side, had a rather formidable character; and his brow, moreover, had that peculiar tension which always impresses one as a sign of a keen impatient temperament.[13]

What George Eliot is presenting in these three characters, with their combination of keenness and mildness, the balance in them of head and heart is, as I have suggested, a concept of maturity— what a fully developed human personality is, or rather ought to be,

11. See I, 106, 107, 232.
12. II, 52; see also I, 110, 327, and II, 286.
13. I, 349–350; see also I, 353.

like.[14] But none of the book's major characters—neither Hetty nor
Adam nor Dinah—belongs at first with Mr. Irwine, Bartle Massey,
and Mrs. Poyser, though some of them eventually join that company. How difficult the task and how valuable its achievement
Adam Bede demonstrates.

II

Hetty Sorrel, as her name suggests, is a perfect representative of
the Loamshire-Hayslope world: she has its fertility, and she has its
beauty, which nevertheless conceals an essential hardness. To think
of Hetty as she first appears in the book is to think of her as being
in certain places, themselves microcosms of Loamshire: the Hall
Farm dairy, its garden, and the Grove of the Donnithorne estate.
Each of these places has an individual aura, but all are suggestive
(with their associated imagery of vegetation, light-color, warmth-
coolness, and moisture) of fertility and growth. To each place
Hetty is linked not only by her presence but also by parallel
imagery: she too is described in terms of vegetation (flowers and
fruit in particular), of light-color, warmth-coolness, and moisture.

Furthermore, each of these places is appropriate to a particular
phase of Hetty's involvement with Arthur.[15] Their first tête-à-tête
occurs in the Hall Farm dairy. George Eliot emphasizes its cleanli-
ness and purity, but it remains, by virtue of its own nature and the
associated imagery, subtly sexualized. More explicitly so is the setting
for the rendezvous between Arthur and Hetty which takes place in
the Grove of the Donnithorne estate. George Eliot describes "a

14. This concept owes much, I believe, to George Eliot's knowledge of the ideas
of Ludwig Feuerbach, whose *Das Wesen des Christentums* she had finished
translating in 1854; but it owes just as much to her own experience (particularly
to her relationship with Lewes) and to the general intellectual temper of the
times in which she lived. Since, then, I do not regard the novel as merely fic-
tionalized philosophy, I have chosen to put most of the relevant Feuerbach
material in footnotes. (I should like to acknowledge here my indebtedness to chs.
VIII and IX of Basil Willey's book, *Nineteenth Century Studies: Coleridge to
Matthew Arnold* [London, 1949]; they contain a valuable discussion of the relationship between Feuerbach's ideas and the fiction of George Eliot.)

15. George Eliot is equally skilful in her handling of the seasonal back-
grounds, which subtly reinforce this same progression and which confirm the
book's major theme.

wood of beeches and limes, with here and there a light, silver-stemmed birch—just the sort of wood most haunted by the nymphs: you see their white sunlit limbs gleaming athwart the boughs . . . you hear their soft liquid laughter—but if you look with a too curious sacrilegious eye, they vanish behind the silvery beeches, they make you believe that their voice was only a running brooklet. . . . It was not a grove with measured grass or rolled gravel . . . but with narrow, hollow-shaped, earthy paths, edged with faint dashes of delicate moss." [16]

When Adam comes to deliver the letter in which Arthur writes that he and Hetty must no longer think of themselves as lovers, Adam finds her in the garden of the Hall Farm. Here, in this "leafy, flowery, bushy time," all things grow together in "careless, half-neglected abundance" (I, 327). One sees "tall hollyhocks beginning to flower, and dazzle the eye with their pink, white, and yellow . . . syringas and Gueldres roses, all large and disorderly for want of trimming . . . leafy walls of scarlet beans and late peas . . . a row of bushy filberts in one direction, and in another a huge apple-tree making a barren circle under its low-spreading boughs. But what signified a barren patch or two?" (I, 327–328). It is appropriate of course that Hetty should be found among the hollyhocks and roses (herself so frequently described in terms of flowers, roses in particular).[17] But if the floweriness and fertility of the place are appropriate, so too is its rankness—growth without order or control.

A second link between Hetty and the Loamshire world is that of her beauty. It was, George Eliot writes, "a spring-tide beauty; . . . the beauty of young frisking things, round-limbed, gambolling, circumventing you by a false air of innocence—the innocence of a young star-browed calf . . . that . . . leads you a severe steeple-chase over hedge and ditch, and only comes to a stand in the middle of a bog" (I, 122–123). Such beauty, at once suggestive of fertility and of the infantile, is difficult to comprehend in its effect: "It is a beauty like that of kittens, or very small downy ducks making gentle rippling noises . . . or babies just beginning to toddle and

16. I, 192; see also passage at I, 193, 194, 196, 201–202.
17. For the latter see in particular I, 279; and 122, 204. For more general flower imagery see I, 196, 236; II, 97. For fruit imagery see I, 314, 325, 329–330.

to engage in conscious mischief—a beauty with which you can never be angry, but that you feel ready to crush for inability to comprehend the state of mind into which it throws you" (I, 121).

It is a false beauty, for it conceals in the case of Hetty a core of hardness, as does the beauty of Loamshire itself. In this respect, if on a different social level, she is similar to Mrs. Irwine or to the squire, and it is significant that those who are like her see only her beauty: Mrs. Irwine, for example, laments the fact that it " 'should be thrown away among the farmers' " (I, 413). But Mrs. Poyser is not deceived. She says that Hetty's heart is as hard as a pebble (I, 233) and that " 'things take no more hold on her than if she was a dried pea' " (II, 75). She is no better " 'than a peacock, as 'ud strut about on the wall, and spread its tail when the sun shone if all the folks i' the parish was dying' " (I, 232), or " 'no better nor a cherry wi' a hard stone inside it.' " [18]

Hetty's hardness is that of childish or at best adolescent egocentricity: all people and events have value or significance only as they impinge upon the narrow circle of her own life; failing that, they are of no importance. At the news of Mr. Bede's death, for example, Hetty is concerned only as long as she thinks it is Adam who is meant; when she discovers her error, she lapses into indifference. She cares little about the Hall Farm, and although dutiful toward her aunt and uncle, she exhibits no real affection for them. Totty, who serves so well as a measure of Mrs. Poyser's love, is an equally good measure of Hetty's inability to love—anyone besides herself, that is. Indeed, there is a muted but persistent strain of autoeroticism in her: one thinks of her inordinate love of fine clothes and adornment,[19] and of such scenes as those in which she appears as the "devout worshipper" before a mirror (I, 223, ff.) and in which she turns up the sleeves of her dress and kisses her own arms "with the passionate love of life" (II, 149). Even her love for Arthur is tinged with the same quality: in him she finds, for a brief time at least, the objectification of her day-dreaming desires, but

18. II, 75 (see also I, 229); for similar verdicts by Mrs. Bede and Bartle Massey see I, 63 and II, 195.

19. Clothing imagery is particularly plentiful in connection with Hetty; see I, 139, 230, 279; II, 74. On Hetty's love of finery and adornment see I, 335, f., 374–378.

these in turn are only the projection in fantasy of her own ego, sexually translated. What she loves in him is not so much Arthur as her own self—as she wishes it might be.

Her emotional life is, in fact, a continuous fantasy, as George Eliot suggests with recurring dream and day-dream imagery.[20] That Hetty is forever "taking holiday in dreams of pleasure" (II, 124) from her workaday life is partly accounted for in sociological terms: all the business of life was managed for her; which in turn is only another way of saying that the Loamshire world (so sheltered and sheltering) has for personalities like those of Hetty and Arthur, which lack energy and will, the fatal power of keeping them forever children. Much of the tragedy—or catastrophe—of both Hetty and Arthur springs from the fact that they are wilful children performing adult actions in an age which is not golden;[21] rather, to change the reference, it is a post-lapsarian world in which actions are neither innocent nor without consequences. Yet Loamshire is sufficiently close to being an "earthly paradise" that at times its inhabitants learn the truth only when it is too late. In one sense, therefore, Hetty is the victim as well as representative of the Loamshire world.

All of this Dinah recognizes when, early in the story, she tries to prepare Hetty for the possibility of pain in life, for the necessity of leaving her adolescent dreamworld, of growing up. Couching her ideas in terms of the troubles that are " 'appointed for us all here below' " (I, 239), she speaks in much the same vein as she had in her sermon on the green. Like the villagers, however, Hetty remains deaf and for the same reasons: her world has never given her any evidence of the existence of suffering; or if it has, then in such fashion as to show that misery always comes to someone outside the sheltered protection of family or community. Thus her reaction to Dinah's words, like that of the villagers, is minimal—only a "chill fear" (I, 240) which remains vague and child-like.

Small wonder that Hetty's awakening has traumatic force. When she learns in a letter from Arthur of his determination to bring their affair to an end, all vitality is drained out of her: her face

20. See, for example, I, 146, 197, 241, 408; II, 46, 47.
21. See I, 193, 228.

becomes blanched (II, 66), she feels "cold and sick and trembling."
Even the light of day fails to cheer her, for it has become "dreary"
(II, 67) to her in her "dry-eyed morning misery." (II, 68). Hetty's
suffering is subsequently compounded by the knowledge that she is
pregnant. Dread of disgrace and censure forces her to flee Loamshire, and in so doing she leaves for the first time a garden world
and enters a wasteland.

The reinforcing imagery George Eliot uses in presenting the
account of Hetty's trip to Windsor and back is skilfully handled.
The time of year is February, early spring by Loamshire standards,
but a spring without hope or promise. All the light and warmth
of the earlier spring-summer world, with its flowers and fruit, hay
and ripening grain are gone, and in their place bleak grayness.
Instead of images of shelter and containment, security and enclosure, George Eliot now uses those of the city, with its baffling
maze of streets, of the long unending road, and of barren open
fields.[22] Much of Hetty's trip is made through rainy weather. She
finds herself subject to coarse comments and is taken for a wild
woman and beggar (II, 150–152). Even the respite she knows at the
inn in Windsor is only like that of a man who throws "himself on
the sand, instead of toiling onward under the scorching sun" (II,
135).

The effect of Hetty's ordeal is to externalize the hardness which
hitherto has been concealed. Although at first her pregnancy had
brought about a sudden burgeoning of "womanliness" (II, 105),
when she bears the child and then (if unintentionally) kills it, she
turns emotionally almost to stone.[23] Mr. Irwine reports the change
to Adam, who sees it for himself at Hetty's trial: she is now a "pale,
hard-looking culprit." [24]

22. Cf. Ludwig Feuerbach, *The Essence of Christianity*, trans., Marian Evans,
2nd ed. (London, 1881), p. 64 (hereafter referred to as Feuerbach, *Essence*): "He
who has an aim has a law over him; he does not merely guide himself; he is
guided. He who has no aim, has no home, no sanctuary; aimlessness is the
greatest unhappiness. Even he who has only common aims [e.g., Chad's Bess]
gets on better, though he may not be better, than he who has no aim."
23. Cf. Hetty's account of returning to the place where she had left the baby:
" 'but when I saw it was gone, I was struck like a stone, with fear. . . . My
heart went like a stone' " (II, 252).
24. II, 216–217; see also II, 96, 145, 241.

Most of the Loamshire world is appalled by the hardness Hetty exhibits, seeing how it has made something inhuman of her. Few of them realize, however, how much they are implicated in her condition; nor can any of them actually help Hetty, since they are unwilling either to forgive or comfort her. But Dinah, the outsider from Stonyshire, where forgiving love can exist because suffering is known, is able to restore Hetty to humanity—to a better humanity, at least, than that with which she had been endowed by her own world.

For the scene of regeneration George Eliot takes us, through ever-increasing darkness, into the deep interior of the prison, where in a tiny stone cell (a fine objective correlative for Hetty's heart) she has Dinah confront Hetty. No attempt of Dinah's to get Hetty to speak is at first effective; she remains as unresponsive as a stone. Finally Dinah resorts to prayer. In it the two dominant images of the chapter—hardness and darkness—merge: Dinah calls upon the Lord to take away the darkness enveloping Hetty and to melt the hardness of her heart. The prayer is efficacious. Hetty is led to confess,[25] spilling forth the whole pitiable tale of her journey in the wasteland, of bearing the child, and then, because she wanted so desperately to return to the world from which the fact of illegitimate life exiled her, leaving the baby in a shallow hole covered with leaves and chips in the hope that someone would find it. The confession, a sufficiently damning account of Hetty herself, is no less damning of the Loamshire world: " 'I daredn't go back home again —I couldn't bear it. I couldn't have bore to look at anybody, for they'd have scorned me.' " [26] Dinah, however, does not scorn her but with loving sympathy comforts her. This is Hetty's regeneration.

In all frankness it is not much of a regeneration, particularly when compared with that of Adam or even of Arthur; for although Hetty is no longer hard, is able to ask Adam's forgiveness, and is willing in turn to forgive Arthur, the only new life she faces is that

25. George Eliot's ideas on the power of confession to relieve suffering echo Feuerbach (among others); cf. the following: "The word has power to redeem, to reconcile, to bless, to make free. The sins which we confess are forgiven us by virtue of the divine power of the word. . . . The forgiveness of sins lies in the confession of sins" (*Essence*, p. 79).

26. II, 247–248; see also II, 138, 139, 152.

of exile. Pardoned from execution, she is nevertheless transported
to the colonies, where she dies some years later. George Eliot might
just as well have had her hanged to begin with.[27] As a matter of fact
it is at this point that Hetty becomes the victim of her creator; for
after all allowance has been made, one is still left with the impres-
sion that toward the kittenish Hetty there is some of the same hardness in George Eliot she deplored in others. That there could be
no room for Hetty in Loamshire is, from a symbolic point of view,
bad enough; that apparently there could be no room for her anywhere in George Eliot's scheme of things stands as an indictment
against the ethic which the book suggests.

III

It is not possible to argue, I believe, that Adam Bede is a perfect
human being, fully mature in George Eliot's terms, from the beginning. This is not so. Intelligent, diligent, trustworthy, loyal he may
be—a veritable Boy Scout—but not yet a man. He is a long way at
first from being an Irwine, a Bartle Massey, or even a masculine
counterpart of Mrs. Poyser. Rather, because in him the head monstrously outweighs the heart, he is kin to sharp old Mrs. Irwine,
the icily polite Squire Donnithorne, and the Martin Poyser made
implacable by slovenly husbandry and erring nieces. Like them he
may possess a full measure of keenness,[28] but he does not even have
Poyser's jolly exterior: Adam is wrathful (I, 56, 58), stern (I, 142),
" 'stiff an' masterful' " (I, 180), unyielding (I, 250; II, 320), harsh
(I, 435; II, 25), hot and hasty (II, 258), intolerant (I, 12), and essentially humorless (I, 6–7, 8).

Whenever, in George Eliot's moral world, there is such an im-
balance of head and heart, the keenness is in danger of turning into
hardness and pride. About Adam's pride there is little disagreement;

27. On a literal level the punishment is not severe (Mary Voce, the original
Hetty, was hanged promptly enough); but I still believe that on the level of
moral and psychological symbolism it is exceedingly harsh (for a differing judgment see A. J. Fyfe, "The Interpretation of *Adam Bede*," *Nineteenth-Century
Fiction*, IX [September 1954], 136).

28. George Eliot uses this word itself frequently in describing Adam (see I,
5, 61, 70, 145, 171, 172, 319; II, 10, 156; see also I, 160 and II, 318).

we hear of it on all sides and are given frequent examples of it.[29] The same is true of Adam's hardness, which consists in his having "too little fellow-feeling with the weakness that errs in spite of foreseen consequences. Without this fellow-feeling," George Eliot continues, "how are we to get enough patience and charity towards our stumbling, falling companions in the long and changeful journey?" (I, 316) The answer, implicit in the first part of *Adam Bede*, is that we do not. Repeatedly in the opening chapters of the book we see Adam, proudly in control of his own life, losing all patience with lesser mortals who stumble and fall—like his own father, for example. The function of old Thias Bede as a character is, indeed, precisely that of revealing the extent of his son's hardness. The same is true of Arthur (in part at least). Toward both men Adam is unforgiving, and even when he repents of his severity, the repentance is futile because it reflects no genuine increase in his capacity for sympathy.[30]

The reason is that Adam is not fully involved emotionally with either his father or Arthur. Because this is so, he can neither participate in their plight nor understand it. What is necessary for Adam (and here George Eliot permits herself the luxury of writing a prescription) is that he get "his heartstrings bound round the weak and erring, so that he must share not only the outward consequence of their error, but their inward suffering" (I, 316). Precisely such an emotional involvement exists for Adam in his relationship with Hetty—a bad one rationally, according to the head (as his mother points out at every opportunity). But this relationship is not a rational one; rather it is a passion which overmasters him. Adam's heartstrings are bound fast to Hetty. George Eliot has seen to that.

Having provided Adam with this full involvement, she next makes certain that he will suffer as a result,[31] first by having him learn that Arthur is Hetty's accepted lover; next by having him think Hetty has run away from their approaching marriage; and finally by having him learn of Hetty's being brought to trial in Stoniton for the murder of her child. There is plenty of suffering

29. See I, 21, 69, 150, 366–367, 406.
30. See I, 303–304.
31. The necessity for Adam to suffer before he can truly love, or even become a man, is pure Feuerbach (see *Essence,* p. 54; see also pp. 59, 62).

here, but Adam's response is different from that of Hetty: where she sank into stasis, he goes in the opposite direction toward violent action. Hetty fell below the level even of human craving; Adam lusts for revenge.[32] The response of both is in keeping with their characters: Hetty, whose hardness is that of selfishness, has no will at all; faced with a situation she cannot handle, she is brought to a dead halt. Adam, whose hardness is that of pride, is all active will, and he lashes out. But the fierce desire for activity does nothing to mitigate his suffering, the marks of which, as in the case of Hetty, are revealed in the changes in his physical appearance.[33]

At this nadir there is yet the possibility, in terms of the novel, for regeneration through a human agent exercising the power of love. Adam's suffering is indeed a precondition for his regeneration. The agent is a double one: Mr. Irwine and Bartle Massey. Both men, themselves fully mature (with their balanced keenness and mildness), do what they can to help Adam in his misery. Sensing in him a potentiality for violence and a desire to take vengeance on Arthur, they seek to divert him. Irwine uses the power of reason, arguing that to injure Arthur will not help Hetty and that passionate violence will lead only to another crime (II, 202–207). Adam agrees, but it is acquiescence, not full acceptance. The latter is brought about by Bartle Massey.

The scene takes place in Stoniton in what George Eliot pointedly calls "an upper room," a "dull upper room." [34] These words have an echoic power and intentionally so, I believe: Adam, who in this scene comes to comprehend the necessity for compassion and forgiveness in life and thereby achieves what George Eliot calls an awakening to "full consciousness" (II, 209), participates in a kind of Lord's Supper—a symbolic one of the sort Feuerbach describes in *The Essence of Christianity*.[35] Before reporting the latest news

32. See II, 184, 197, 208.

33. See II, 168, 200, 216, 266–267.

34. After the scene between Adam and Bartle the echoic language is dropped; the room thenceforth is referred to merely as "Adam's room" (II, 253) and "that small chamber" (II, 257).

35. Cf., for example, the following: "The sacrament of Faith is Baptism, the sacrament of Love is the Lord's Supper" (*Essence*, p. 236). And: "If in water we adore the pure force of Nature, in bread and wine we adore the supernatural power of mind, of consciousness, of man. Hence this sacrament is only for man matured into consciousness; while baptism is imparted to infants" (p. 277).

of the trial Bartle says. " 'I must see to your having a bit of the loaf, and some of that wine Mr Irwine sent this morning. . . . I must have a bit and a sup myself. Drink a drop with me, my lad—drink with me' " (II, 210–211). Throughout the scene, as Bartle tells his news, he urges Adam to partake: " 'You must show courage. Drink some wine now, and show me you mean to bear it like a man' " (II, 212). At first Adam's thoughts continue to play bitterly on his own suffering and his desire for revenge, but gradually, as Bartle speaks, his hardness melts,[36] and finally he declares that he will go to the court and stand by Hetty, that her own flesh and blood were cowardly to cast her off. To which Bartle replies: " 'Take a bit, then, and another sup, Adam, for the love of me. See, I must stop and eat a morsel. Now, you take some.' Nerved by an active resolution, Adam took a morsel of bread, and drank some wine. He was haggard and unshaven, as he had been yesterday, but he stood upright again, and looked more like the Adam Bede of former days" (II, 214).

Adam's decision to stand by Hetty, an expression of his old love for her as well as of his new willingness to involve his life with the suffering of others, has two consequences: it leads to his being able to forgive Arthur, and it makes him capable of a new sort of love (Feuerbach describes it when he writes: "Love does not exist without sympathy, sympathy does not exist without suffering in common" [*Essence*, p. 54]). For many the love which subsequently grows between Dinah and Adam (as well as their marriage) seems an anticlimax. While granting that George Eliot has some difficulty in focusing the conclusion, I cannot agree that it is an "artistic weakness," as Henry James would have it:[37] without it one is left with two of the principal figures—Adam and Dinah—still incomplete human beings. That this is so with Adam is clearly demonstrable: he has lost his hardness; by suffering he has become compassionate and therefore capable of loving; but he does not yet love. Without love there can be no fulfillment of personality.

The charge, however, that Dinah is an incomplete human being may well seem outrageous; but she too, I believe, lacks something

36. II, 214; see also II, 258. For the effect of his decision upon Adam's appearance see II, 253, 254, 266–267.
37. *Partial Portraits*, "The Life of George Eliot" (London, 1888), p. 53.

at the beginning of the story, for despite her mildness[38] and compassion, her selflessness and love of God, she has little genuine vitality. Dinah is all heart.[39] She scarcely seems to breathe in the midst of her enduring calm and takes little or no nourishment—only scant victuals, as Mrs. Poyser would say. Confronted by a vigorous fruitful world, she retreats. The cause of her retreat is the fear of selfishness and hardness resulting from too great abundance of worldly goods. This much, at least, Dinah says herself.

Implicit in her fear is also, I believe, a kind of unwillingness to become fully involved in life. In this respect she is like her creator, who once said that it was a pity her life could not be managed for her, while she stood by, the passive but interested spectator. Just such a one is Dinah: she observes the human condition, with sympathy and compassion, it is true, but without involvement.[40] Selfless is a word used frequently in describing her, but selfless means not only something different from selfish; it means also lacking in self. To lack this sense of human identity is to become something either less or more than human—a clod, perhaps, or a divinity. Talking of herself to Mr. Irwine, she says:

> "I'm too much given to sit still and keep by myself: it seems as if I could sit silent all day long with the thought of God overflowing my soul—as the pebbles lie bathed in the Willow Brook. For thoughts are so great—aren't they, sir? They seem to lie upon us like a deep flood; and it's my besetment to forget where I am and

38. See II, 207, 254, 296; see also II, 27.

39. Cf. Feuerbach's account of an adequate concept of God and, by extension, an adequate concept of man: "If a God without feeling, without a capability of suffering, will not suffice to man as a feeling, suffering being, neither will a God with feeling only, a God without intelligence and *will* [italics mine]. Only a being who comprises in himself the whole man can satisfy the whole man" (*Essence,* p. 65). Cf. also the following: "But love [heart] with understanding [head] and understanding with love is mind, and mind is the totality of man as such—the total man" (p. 67).

40. Cf. Feuerbach, *Essence:* "It is pleasanter to be passive than to act, to be redeemed and made free by another than to free oneself; pleasanter to make one's salvation dependent on a person than on the force of one's own spontaneity; pleasanter to set before oneself an object of love than an object of effort; pleasanter to know oneself beloved by God than merely to have that simple, natural selflove which is innate in all beings . . . pleasanter, in short, to allow oneself to be acted on by one's own feeling, as by another, but yet fundamentally identical being, than to regulate oneself by reason" (p. 140).

everything about me, and lose myself in thoughts that I could give no account of, for I could neither make a beginning nor ending of them in words." [41]

Such a state represents a complete withdrawal from life, and withdrawal (or retreat) is characteristic of Dinah. Whenever the going gets rough, that is, whenever life begins, paradoxically, to seem too pleasant and seductive, Dinah flees—back to Stonyshire, barren and sterile under the "overarching sky." [42] The most notable of these strategic retreats occurs after Adam has told her of his love. Following his declaration, Dinah replies that she could return his love save for the fear that she would " 'forget to rejoice and weep with others,' " even forget the divine presence (II, 333). Her peace and joy come from having no life of her own. Adam's love only raises the fear that she will forget Jesus, the man of sorrows, and become hard: " 'And think how it is with me, Adam:—that life I have led is like a land I have trodden in blessedness since my childhood; and if I long for a moment to follow the voice which calls me to another land that I know not, I cannot but fear that my soul might hereafter yearn for that early blessedness which I had forsaken; and where doubt enters there is not perfect love. I must wait for clearer guidance: I must go from you' " (II, 337). Here is clear expression of Dinah's fear of accepting full maturity; for the land which faces her (i.e., Loamshire and, of course, Adam) is a strange one, and who knows what life there may hold for her? Better, then, to return to the other land (Stonyshire and the self-contained world of childhood). There at least no risk is run. If Hetty was incapable of growing up, Dinah is afraid to.

We are not permitted to see the process by which Dinah is enabled to overcome her fear, and it is a serious flaw in the novel that is so. All we learn is that having been told by Adam of his love for her and having admitted in turn a love for him, Dinah once more retreats to Stonyshire, not staying even long enough to

41. I, 131; cf. Feuerbach, *Essence:* "The heart, however, does not invent in the same way as the free imagination or intelligence; it has a passive, receptive relation to what it produces; all that proceeds from it seems to it given from without, takes it by violence, works with the force of irresistible necessity. The heart overcomes, masters man; he who is once in its power is possessed as it were by his demon, by his God" (p. 59).

42. See Dinah's comments, I, 132.

participate in the Harvest Supper. Adam, after waiting for several weeks, is no longer able to endure the strain and sets out for Stony-shire to find her. As he leaves the Loamshire world and enters gray treeless Stonyshire, he is reminded of the painful past, but in an altered light, for he possesses what George Eliot calls a "sense of enlarged being" (II, 365), the consequence of the fuller life brought about by his suffering. He sees Stonyshire now through Dinah's eyes, as it were, and if his vision includes the barren land, it also includes the wonderful flooding light and the large embracing sky.

Adam waits for Dinah to return from her Sunday preaching not at her home, but on a hill top. Here, in the midst of her world, he discovers that Dinah has undergone a change: the power of her love for him has in a sense overcome her fears; she feels like a divided person without him, and she is willing to become his wife (II, 367–369). He therefore takes her back to Loamshire, whence she had so precipitately fled. It is not, however, to the green and golden world of June with which the book began; rather, to an autumnal mature world. Here, "on a rimy morning in departing November" (II, 370), when there is a tinge of sadness in the weather as well as in the joy which accompanies the wedding, Adam and Dinah are married. And it is fitting that the hint of sorrow should be present, for in the world which George Eliot reveals to us, life not only contains sorrow, it needs sorrow in order that there may be love. That this discovery is a rare one George Eliot suggests: nothing, she writes, "like Dinah and the history which had brought her and Adam Bede together had been known at Hayslope within the memory of man" (II, 371). That it was also for George Eliot a profoundly meaningful discovery we may gather from the now famous question: "Shall I ever write another book as true as 'Adam Bede'?" [43]

43. This article was completed before the appearance of Maurice Hussey's "Structure and Imagery in *Adam Bede*" (*Nineteenth-Century Fiction*, X [September 1955], 115–129). While much that Mr. Hussey says would obviously have been of value in preparing this article, and although we occasionally reach similar conclusions, our points of view are sufficiently different that serious overlapping does not, I believe, occur.

Intelligence as Deception:
The Mill on the Floss

by George Levine

With only small exceptions, *The Mill on the Floss* can be seen as adequately representative of even the most mature of George Eliot's art—morally energetic yet unsentimentally perceptive about the meaning of experience. Like all of her works, it is thoroughly coherent and gains its coherence from a unified vision. But the vision, here as elsewhere, is, I would argue, incomplete. There were elements in experience, that is, which she was never fully able to assimilate and which, as was true of most of the major Victorian writers, she was genuinely unable to see. She pushed the boundaries of Victorian experience as far as any of her contemporaries and moved to the brink from which one can observe the modern sensibility, but inevitably she pulled back.

The point at which she stopped is the point at which *The Mill on the Floss*—which remains one of the very great novels of the period—goes wrong. The difficulty, I would suggest, is not merely George Eliot's excessive moral energy nor even, exclusively, her too close identification, criticised by F. R. Leavis, with her heroine.[1]

"Intelligence as Deception: The Mill on the Floss" by George Levine. From *Publications of the Modern Language Association of America.* LXXX (September, 1965), 402–9. Copyright © 1965 by the Modern Language Association of America. Reprinted by permission of the Modern Language Association of America.

1. See *The Great Tradition* (New York: Anchor Books, 1954), p. 58. "In George Eliot's presentment of Maggie there is an element of self-idealisation." This is obviously, but only partially, true. Indeed, the whole thematic development of the book depends on a careful rendering of Maggie's limitations. See in this connection Jerome Thale's note on Maggie in *The Novels of George Eliot*

Rather, it seems to me to result from a complex mode of self-deceit
—from a combination of high intelligence with powerful moral
revulsion from what that intelligence tended to reveal.

I

It is important, at the outset, to remember that George Eliot's
intelligence was at home with several highly elaborated intellectual
systems which, she believed, could largely—if not entirely—account
for the experience being narrated. Of course, her works cannot be
reduced simply to any one set of rationally coherent ideas; but it
is certainly true that her empirical and rationalist biases (modified
though they were by her total commitment to "truth of feeling")[2]
demanded an explanation of experience consistent with reason,
and that the explanation she accepted influenced certain crucial
elements in her novels.[3] Determinism is the central and dominant
explanation of the facts of the experience; the moral direction of
those facts is controlled largely by many ideas which might be

---

(New York, 1959), and William Steinhoff, "Intent and Fulfillment in the Ending
of *The Mill on the Floss*," in *The Image of the Work* (Berkeley, Calif., 1955),
pp. 231–251. Mr. Steinhoff's analysis runs parallel to my own but does not
overlap. He too, however, emphasizes George Eliot's insistence on Maggie's
limitations.

2. George Eliot, like the thinkers she consciously followed, recognized that
feeling not thought was the major source of action and that cultivation of the
intellect without cultivation of the sensibilities was morally dangerous. Her
most famous statement of the notion comes in a fairly early letter: "The first
impulse of a young and ingenuous mind is to withhold the slightest sanction
from all that contains even a mixture of supposed error. . . . But a year or two
of reflection and experience of our own miserable weakness which will ill afford
to part even with the crutches of superstition must, I think, effect a change . . .
and we turn to *truth of feeling* as the only universal bond of union. We find
that the intellectual errors we once fancied were a mere incrustation have grown
into the living body and that we cannot in the majority of cases wrench them
away without destroying vitality" (*The George Eliot Letters,* ed. Gordon S.
Haight, 7 vols., New Haven, 1954–56, I, 162).

3. One of the central concerns of this essay, to trace the relation of the
thematic content of *The Mill on the Floss* to Feuerbach and Comte, was largely
inspired by a brief essay by U. C. Knoepflmacher, "George Eliot, Feuerbach, and
the Question of Criticism," *Victorian Studies,* VII (1964), 306–309. I am also
greatly indebted to Bernard Paris, "George Eliot's Religion of Humanity,"
ELH, XXIX (1962), 418–443.

traced to Comte and Feuerbach.[4] All of these ideas are woven inextricably into the very texture of *The Mill on the Floss,* but I shall argue that there came a recognizable point at which, especially in her use of Feuerbach, George Eliot employs them in such a way as to help her escape the implications of her own most deeply felt insights.

To begin with, then, it is necessary to clarify what the informing ideas of *The Mill on the Floss* meant to George Eliot. For her, determinism, as I have explained elsewhere,[5] entailed a total commitment to the notion that every action has its causes, and only by a meticulous examination of those causes can any action be seen as comprehensible. She also argued, however, that determinism does not entail belief in inefficacy of the will. Since, that is, a man's character is always an element in his choice, he must be seen as responsible. Finally, whatever the intellectual formulation might be, to excuse a man on the basis of an abstract theory of determinism is altogether irrelevant to his evil; as Adam Bede remarks, "I see plain enough we shall never do it without a resolution, and that's enough for me." [6]

All the major themes of *The Mill on the Floss,* as well as its structure, are related to determinism. It is a commonplace that the novel develops as Tom and Maggie grow: it sets them within the framework of a family and society which extensively determine what they become, shows the inevitable development of their characters according to the pressures of heredity and irrevocable events, and traces their destinies chronologically from love, to division, to

4. For a useful and compact survey of the relation of the ethical ideas of Comte and Feuerbach to those of George Eliot, I am indebted to the fourth chapter of Michael Wolff's unpublished doctoral dissertation, "Marian Evans to George Eliot: The Moral and Intellectual Foundation of her Career," microfilm (Princeton, 1958). It should be noted here that determinism has moral implications of its own and is an element of Positivism. John Stuart Mill goes so far as to say that "Whoever regards all events as part of a constant order, each one being the invariable consequent of some antecedent condition, or combination of conditions, accepts fully the Positive mode of thought" (*Auguste Comte and Positivism,* Ann Arbor, Mich., 1961, p. 15).

5. "Determinism and Responsibility in the Works of George Eliot," *PMLA,* LXXVII (1962), 268–279.

6. *Adam Bede,* ch. xvii. All quotations from George Eliot's works, unless otherwise noted, are from the Cabinet Edition, 24 vols. (London and Edinburgh, n.d.).

unity in death. The simple narrative progression is incremental and stresses the ineluctable dependence of every act and thought on acts and thoughts which preceded them.

Both in its personal drama and in its vividly imagined description of a period of social transition the novel seems illustrative also of many of Comte's and Feuerbach's notions of social and moral growth. In a letter to John Blackwood comparing *Adam Bede* to *The Mill on the Floss,* which was then in progress, George Eliot noted that the characters in the latter "are on a lower level generally." [7] Quite deliberately, she was creating a society which has not as yet moved beyond the egoism of man's animal beginnings to the sympathy and benevolence which Feuerbach and Comte believed would grow out of egoism. Among other things, the frequency with which all the characters are compared to insects and animals makes plain that George Eliot does not see them as ready for any but the slightest advance toward the full intellectual and moral development from egoism to intelligent sympathy towards which she aspired.

Aside from working out George Eliot's characteristic theme of "the adjustment of our individual needs to the dire necessities of our lot," [8] Maggie's story is also a dramatization of Feuerbach's religion of suffering—the "suffering, whether of martyr or victim, which belongs to every historical advance of mankind." [9] Through suffering the "obscure vitality" of the "emmet-like Dodsons and Tullivers" will be transcended, will be "swept into the same oblivion with the generations of ants and beavers," and man will move slowly towards his full humanity. The immersion in water, which in the final chapter is the form which the suffering takes, is, in Feuerbach's

7. *The George Eliot Letters,* III, 133.
8. J. W. Cross, *George Eliot's Life,* Bk. III, ch. xv.
9. *The Mill on the Floss,* Bk. IV, ch. i. All quotations from this novel will be from Gordon S. Haight's careful edition (Boston: Riverside Editions, 1961). See Feuerbach's *Essence of Christianity,* transl. George Eliot (New York: Harper Torchbooks, 1957): "Man has the consciousness not only of a spring of activity, but also of a spring of suffering in himself. I feel; and I feel feeling (not merely will and thought, which are only too often in opposition to me and my feelings), as belonging to my essential being, and, though the source of all sufferings and sorrows, as a glorious divine power and perfection" (p. 63). It is, by the way, precisely the unity of thought and feeling, with feeling predominating, which Comte aspired towards. See Comte's *A General View of Positivism,* transl. J. H. Bridges (Stanford: Academic Reprints, n.d.), and Wolff, pp. 204–211.

view, an annihilation of consciousness: it is the first step towards regeneration, but the regeneration itself must be active, not passive, the assertion of "the power of mind, of consciousness, of man." [10] Maggie's world lacks the moral guidance Comte insisted was necessary for that regeneration or for the achievement of a satisfactory society: it had "no standard but hereditary custom" (Bk. IV, ch. i).

Ideas such as these form the intellectual framework of *The Mill on the Floss*. The ideas and the experience, however, are two aspects of the same thing. Here at least one feels no tension between the two halves of the almost schizophrenic (intellectual vs. emotional) George Eliot that critics have taken to creating. For all but a brief section of the book the experience itself seems a necessary and convincing source of the ideas; although the world the novel describes is entirely deterministic and largely positivistic, the "system" does not distort the experience. But since the details of the novel are so widely known, I shall concentrate on the relation between the ideas and the experience—rather than on the experience itself—in order to suggest how George Eliot's extraordinarily tough-minded and complicated analysis of personal and social experience could have concluded in a "comfortingly conventional" way, "its tone barely distinguishable from hundreds of pious and exemplary tales where salvation comes through sacrifice and love triumphs over death." [11]

II

George Eliot's "love of the childhood scenes" [12] is not likely to have carried her to such lengthy description as we have in the early books had she not felt those scenes were important, both intrinsically and for the development of the novel as a whole. They are in fact a demonstration of the idea which she found confirmed in Comte, of whom she said that "no one has more clearly seen the truth, that the past rules the present, lives in it, and that we are but the

10. Feuerbach, p. 277.
11. Miriam Allott, "George Eliot in the 1860's," *Victorian Studies,* V (1961), 105.
12. See her now famous statement: "My love of the childhood scenes made me linger over them; so that I could not develop as fully as I wished the concluding book in which the tragedy occurs, and which I had looked forward to with attentive premeditation from the beginning" (*The George Eliot Letters,* III, 374).

growth and outcome of the past." [13] The focus on family in the first book relates directly to the Comtean notion (shared by Feuerbach) that the family is the primary means by which man can transcend his egoism and animality.[14] These early scenes establish that the characters are, in Feuerbach's terms, in a "natural" state, beneath the level of full humanity. It is no accident, for example, that the novel's first speech by an important character—Mr. Tulliver—should begin, "What I want," nor that George Eliot should pointedly repeat the clause (Bk. i, ch. ii). "The oppressive narrowness" of the Dodsons and Tullivers creates a tension for both readers and characters. On the one hand, it is what must be transcended by Maggie if she is to rise above "the mental level of the generation before" her. On the other, she is tied to that generation "by the strongest fibres of" her heart. In "the onward tendency of human things" the Dodsons and Tullivers must go, but they cannot be ignored and they must, indeed, be loved (see Bk. iv, ch. i).

The notions explicit in this view suggest how the story points towards both personal and social growth; and these notions are worked out in almost every detail of the novel. The town of St. Ogg's, to use only one example, has grown in a slow, incremental, entirely unplanned way. It has roots deep in the past, and every part of it is "familiar with forgotten years." Under the slow pressure of time the processes of cause and effect have built it, almost as a natural growth. And George Eliot certainly means to imply a parallel between social and natural law which is central to the beliefs we have been examining:

> It is one of those old, old towns which impress one as a continuation and outgrowth of nature, as much as the nests of the bowerbirds or the winding galleries of the white ants: a town which carries the traces of its long growth and history like a millennial tree, and has sp.ung up and developed in the same spot between the river and the low hill from the time when the Roman legions turned their backs on it from the camp on the hillside, and the long-haired sea-kings came up the river and looked with fierce eager eyes at the fatness of the land (Bk. i, ch. xii).

13. *The George Eliot Letters*, iii, 320.
14. See Wolff, pp. 214–215.

Even the architecture suggests the natural connections with the primitive sea-kings; equally, the citizens of St. Ogg's are what they are because of the past: inconsistent, old-fashioned, egocentric, crude, but sympathetic because they inherit—even without being aware of it—the best (along with the worst) of what men have thought and felt. But because they lack the clarity of vision Feuerbach desiderated they are determined: they "inherited a long past without thinking of it" (Bk. 1, ch. xii).

The Dodsons and Tullivers, of course, are the dramatic embodiments of the town's essential nature, and they confirm the notion that for George Eliot determinism is both dangerous and morally essential. She saw with Feuerbach that society included not merely rigid conventions but also the slowly, painfully earned developments in man's intelligence and sensibility. Maggie, then, must learn what other characters suffer by not learning—that everything must be judged on its unique merits, that no laws, habits, or traditions can apply indiscriminately in all situations. On the other hand, much of what she does learn in this way turns out to be a "relearning" of the values already implicit in social conventions. The trouble with the Dodsons and Tullivers is that they fail to establish an adequate relation to their own traditions and are therefore unable to understand their own motives derived from myriad causes out of the past. Neither they nor Maggie quite attain the "objectivity" Feuerbach requires, the ability, that is, to see "the real relation of things." [15] They cannot achieve that "right understanding" of "the unchangeable Order of the world" which Comte says "is the principal object of our actions." [16]

The predominant theme of the novel then, as George Eliot makes explicit, is the quest for unity—social, familial, and personal—that fusion of imagination and will which leads to sympathetic action. A convenient summary of Feuerbach's views will suggest the direction George Eliot wants Maggie's history to take:

> The individual who has a strongly sympathetic nature combined with profound experience and the ability to imagine the inner states of others has a moral life that is independent of traditions; he has a more highly developed conscience and a truer sense of good and evil

15. See Paris, p. 435.
16. Comte, p. 29.

than tradition, in its present state of development, could supply. The sympathetic tendencies can lead a person to rebel against the harsh usages of tradition, even when such rebellion involves great personal risk.[17]

But this combination of qualities, which can lead justifiably to a rebellion against convention, was more George Eliot's than Maggie's. It would not be stretching things to consider the possibility that these views of Feuerbach helped George Eliot justify to herself her decision to live with G. H. Lewes.[18] But Maggie needs yet to unify her desires with her intentions, to discipline her passions in keeping with an objective view of possibility—"knowledge of the irreversible laws within and without her, which, governing the habits, becomes morality, and developing the feelings of submission and dependence, becomes religion" (Bk. IV, ch. iii).

Socially, the quest is for unity between public opinion and individual sensibility. Comte places heavy emphasis on the value of public opinion in a way relevant to *The Mill on the Floss*. "The principal feature of the state to which we are tending," he says, "will be the increased influence which Public Opinion is destined to exercise. It is in this beneficial influence that we shall find the surest guarantee for morality. . . . Except the noblest of joys, that which springs from social sympathy when called into constant exercise, there is no reward for doing right so satisfactory as the approval of our fellow-beings." [19] Maggie's relation to public opinion seems different, but that is partially because the society in which she lives is at such a primitive stage of development. George Eliot is certainly suggesting in the final chapters both the power of public opinion and the need to develop it more consistently to a higher level of social sympathy. The society of St. Ogg's, however, is disintegrating, as Dr. Kenn says, under the pressure of modern life, "seems tending toward the relaxation of ties—towards the substitution of wayward choice for adherence to obligation, which has its roots in the past" (Bk. VII, ch. i).

17. Paris, p. 424.
18. This point is taken up briefly by Basil Willey in *Nineteenth Century Studies* (New York, 1949), p. 228, and Gordon Haight, *George Eliot and John Chapman* (New Haven, 1940), p. 80.
19. Comte, p. 153.

All aspects of the theme of unity are worked out in three of Maggie's moments of choice: her interview with Philip Wakem in the Red Deeps, her rowing party with Stephen Guest, and her refusal to stay with Stephen after they arrive at Mudport. The two earlier decisions show that Maggie has not achieved that personal unity which is essential to moral well-being. Philip is obviously right when, attacking her new-found asceticism, he warns her that if she persists in mere negations she will find that when she is "thrown upon the world . . . every rational satisfaction of your nature that you deny now, will assault you like a savage appetite" (Bk. v, ch. iii). Unfortunately, of course, even this sensible argument serves to weaken Maggie because it is not disinterested, but designed to keep her from leaving Philip altogether. The truth in this case is a lie, and deceit in the complicated deterministic universe of George Eliot is a form of moral disease whose dangers are far-reaching. It may be, as Maggie recognizes, that "it is other people's wrong feelings that make concealment necessary; but concealment is bad, however it may be caused" (Bk. v, ch. iii).

Nor has Maggie achieved unity by the time she meets Stephen Guest. Whatever one's objections to Stephen as a character, it is obvious that here as elsewhere George Eliot has been extremely careful to work out the reason for the action. What Maggie does with Stephen is determined by a past in which egotism and personal wilfulness keep her from moral integrity. There is no need here to list all the causes, but it is interesting to note how down to the finest details it is possible to observe kinship with the thought of Feuerbach and Comte. One of the things, for instance, which attracts Maggie to Stephen is his singing, and Maggie is deeply susceptible to music. Feuerbach argues strongly for the power of music: "What would man be without feeling?" he asks. "It is the musical power in man. But what would man be without music? Just as man has a musical faculty and feels an inward necessity to breathe out his feelings in song; so, by a like necessity, he, in religious sighs and tears, streams forth the nature of feeling as an objective, divine nature." [20] Music, George Eliot remarks, "could hardly be without some intoxicating effect on her, after years of privation." It should be noted also that Maggie's desperate need to be admired and loved,

20. Feuerbach, p. 63.

one of the causes of her fall, corresponds closely to Comte's sense of what makes people behave as they do.

Because Maggie succumbs at her second moment of choice with Stephen, she is faced with a dilemma which is, in some ways, the purest in all of George Eliot's novels. Maggie's decision now cannot be in passive accordance with the push of circumstance; it depends on her understanding of the particular situation and cannot be governed by conventions. Simply by following out the implications of her complex attitudes towards tradition and modernity, self-control and self-assertion, George Eliot here arrives at a point where tradition cannot supply an adequate answer but where her heroine's character is inadequate to the task of Feuerbach's sympathetic re-bellion. Maggie cannot even decide on the basis of the likely consequences of her actions because the damage has already been done and misery will be the consequence of either choice.

Thus, in making this third choice, Maggie achieves the highest level of consciousness of which a St. Ogg's citizen is capable. She reveals an awareness of the "real relation of things" by accepting both the irrevocability of her act and the fact that it "must blot her life" and bring sorrow into lives that were "knit up with hers by trust and love." She is aware that she has broken all "the ties that had given meaning to duty, and had made herself an outlawed soul," having lost the relation to community which, in Comte's sense, provides moral guidance; she was left with "no guide but the wayward choice of her own soul" (Bk. vi, ch. xiv). Recognizing this loss and its dangers, Maggie attempts to turn to the past and inherited traditions. "If the past is not to bind us," she says to Stephen, "where can duty lie: We have not law but the inclination of the moment" (Bk. vi, ch. xiv). Through the past she attempts to overcome the persistent fragmentation of self which has hitherto left her vulnerable to the past's uncomprehended forces.

She struggles against committing herself to a "momentary triumph of my feeling," to an evil which will form a habit of surrender to impulse and fragmentation. One of George Eliot's primary insights, dramatized in the curious passivity of her characters at their moments of choice, is that "character" as it has been formed over a lifetime finally determines how one will behave in a crisis. Untrained will is unequal to the pressures of the moment; the training of the will into a habit of goodness is essential because "moral behavior is only to be found in the spontaneous exercise of moral emotion. Moral action is not the result of a decision to act morally; it is the result of moral feeling, forcing itself into practice." [21] At her present stage of development, Maggie must still labor at her choice, but she does move towards the unity of self which makes moral action a habit by recognizing that mind, memories, obligations are all part of what a man is, fully as important as natural feelings; and she tries to bring her feelings into conformity with her conscious intentions. The renunciation of Stephen moves one step beyond her immature asceticism, not based on a sense of the real relation of things, which Philip had criticized in the Red Deeps.

III

In keeping with her deterministic insistence on the pressure of ordinary events, her Comtean awareness of the moral pressures of public opinion, and the deep psychological perceptions she shared with Feuerbach about the nature of human suffering and morality, George Eliot could not allow Maggie's resolution yet to be final. Resolutions must be tested moment by moment and day by day and they must establish themselves in relation not only to the complete self but to the community. Thus, all the influences so carefully prepared through the apparently leisurely movement of the early stages of the novel come into play in the last book.

The tensions between the Dodsons and the Tullivers—between the two modes of egoism represented by the forces of convention uncomprehended and rigidified and the forces of blind spontaneity of feeling—now become in a more complex way the tensions between Maggie and the town. All of Maggie's past—not understood—contributed to her fatal lapse with Stephen; so all of Maggie's past —now largely if incompletely understood—contributes to her decision to return to St. Ogg's. Equally, all the seemingly innocuous

---

21. Wolff, p. 228. See Feuerbach, p. 321; "To the man of noble feeling, the noble action is natural: he does not place it in the scales of choice; he *must* do it. Only he who acts so is a man to be confided in." Clearly, Maggie never approaches this seemingly instinctive nobility until her last heroic act.

circumstances which precede Maggie's lapse help determine the rigidly conventional—that is, unimaginative and therefore unsympathetic—response of the townspeople to Maggie. In language which suggests the quite conscious influence of both Comte and Feuerbach, George Eliot describes the "ladies of St. Ogg's" as "not beguiled by any wide speculative conceptions; but they had their favourite abstraction called society which seemed to make their consciences perfectly easy in doing what satisfied their egoism" (Bk. VII, ch. iv.). George Eliot's revulsion from abstractions is widely known, and in its temperamental character it is much more akin to Feuerbach than to Comte, who, though he insisted always on the positive and scientific, was himself the victim of abstractions. But this passage certainly evokes Comte, who, according to John Stuart Mill, described the "Metaphysical Stage" of human development as the stage which "accounts for phenomena by ascribing them, not to volitions either sublunary or celestial, but to realized abstractions. In this stage it is no longer a god that causes and directs each of the various agencies of nature: it is a power, or a force, or an occult quality, considered as real existence, inherent in but distinct from concrete bodies in which they reside, and which they in a manner animate." [22]

The traditions animating the kind of Dodsonian behavior which condemns Maggie are given new life and meaning by the eldest of the Dodsons, Mrs. Glegg, who is capable of dealing with new kinds of experience because she is the strongest willed and most intelligent of the clan. Her willingness to oppose public opinion and convention is certainly intended as at least in part a dramatization of the way in which family unity—recognized by both Comte and Feuerbach as the source of morality—is the first step toward community, the first means of transcending the "I" for the "Thou," for breaking away from the narrow egoism which governs the action of ordinary men. It is the source of Maggie's higher sensibility, and as it is revivified in Mrs. Glegg it helps us to understand George Eliot's commitment to the sustaining power of tradition.

Despite Mrs. Glegg's help, however, the pressures on Maggie become strong enough to make her feel again the temptation to return to Stephen. She must once again work out the relation be-

22. Mill, p. 11.

tween self-will and self-denial, and George Eliot's comment on the problem reveals the impasse at which both author and heroine have arrived: "The great problem of the shifting relation between passion and duty is clear to no man who is capable of apprehending it: the question whether the moment has come in which a man has fallen below the possibility of a renunciation that will carry any efficacy, and must accept the sway of passion against which he had struggled as a trespass, is one for which we have no master-key that will fit all cases" (Bk. vii, ch. ii). As the book has demonstrated, only in a society where egoism and self-will are not driven as in Maggie's case into excessive self-denial or, as in Tom's case, into respectability and moral brutality, does the problem of the shifting relation have a chance to be resolved. But such a positivist utopia, in which the individual and society are allied in one will, was, as George Eliot knew, a mere dream of the future,[23] and one could only move towards it through the slow increment of wasted lives, of suffering such as Maggie's and Dorothea Brooke's, from which new moral insight can be assimilated into man's consciousness. Maggie is at an impasse which everything in the book has suggested is unresolvable. And Dr. Kenn's comment that any action she might take would be "clogged with evil" is undeniably true.

IV

The continuity of George Eliot's views is suggested by the similarity between Maggie's conflict as she battles temptation in the dark night preceding the flood and that of Dorothea on the night she resolves to accept Casaubon's unexplained demands. Both characters submit themselves to the higher responsibility despite the loss of the possibility of self-fulfillment. But neither character is made to face the full implications of such renunciation. Certainly, Dorothea does not achieve a fate with Ladislaw equal to her own large possibilities. Moreover, George Eliot means us to understand that her marriage to him will evoke considerable public disapprobation. But she is certainly not at such a primitive stage of development as

23. See her famous letter to Frederic Harrison rejecting his proposal that she write a novel presenting the ideal Positivist community (*The George Eliot Letters,* iv, 300).

Maggie, and Casaubon's death does save her from total and pointless
frustration. This death follows almost immediately after her resolution, just as Maggie's death follows her own final renunciation.

In her first spontaneously moral action, she rushes to Tom's
rescue and is swept to death in his arms, as though one were meant
to see in that death her reconciliation to all those forces to which
she could by temperament and action never be reconciled. Maggie's
final action, however, can be seen as the last stage in the progress
of her growth according to Feuerbach's principle and therefore altogether consistent with what has gone before. Beginning in mere
egoism and rebellion, she moves on to the incomplete sympathy—
as a result of family pressures—of her asceticism; the suffering which
she endures intensifies that sympathy and produces in her a surer
vision of reality so as to make her capable of a deliberate act of
renunciation with Stephen; her rescue of Tom, however, is to be
seen as a spontaneous moral action which suggests the real beginning of Feuerbach's genuinely noble man. But Maggie's newly
earned "nobility" is once again exercised in the direction of her
family, and will, moreover, never be tested in that infinitely more
complicated social world which posed her moral dilemma. The
escape, then, is thematically consistent, but it can be seen also as
external and fortuitous, an intrusion of that "Favourable Chance"
which George Eliot anathematized in *Silas Marner* (ch. ix).

One can only speculate on the reasons for such a lapse, characteristic not only of George Eliot's work but of much of the best
work of the time. Perhaps Matthew Arnold's explanation of why he
removed "Empedocles on Etna" from his 1853 *Poems* will throw
light on the problem. Arnold, it will be remembered, asked with
Schiller for an art "dedicated to Joy," since "there is no higher and
more serious problem, than how to make men happy." George
Eliot, for her part, during the decade following *The Mill on the
Floss*, wrote that "the art which leaves the soul in despair is laming
to the soul, and is denounced by the healthy sentiment of an
active community." [24] She is likely to have agreed with Arnold
that there were certain situations, "from the representation of
which, though accurate, no poetical enjoyment can be derived. They
are those in which the suffering finds no vent in action; in which a

24. Cross, III, xv.

continuous state of mental distress is prolonged, unrelieved by incident, hope, or resistance; in which there is everything to be endured, nothing to be done." [25] This is Maggie's condition before the flood.

For Arnold, the solution was to abandon art for criticism; George Eliot, also too intelligent and too responsible to let need consciously dictate to art, allowed herself to flaw her art, I would suggest, by deceiving herself with her own intelligence. She could, consistently with her own view of experience, avoid the condition Arnold described by leaning on Comte and Feuerbach; and in this way she could give Maggie the heroic, tragic, but largely affirmative action with which she dies. This action is consistent not only with the details of the plot as she carefully worked them out,[26] but with the very themes which give the novel so much of its richness.

Moreover, within the system of Feuerbachian thought, the death by water makes good symbolic sense. Water, for Feuerbach, is one of the two major sacraments, the other and more important one being the bread and wine of the Lord's Supper. But although, as has been shown, much symbolic use of this sacrament occurs in *Adam Bede*[27] there is apparently no such use in *The Mill on the Floss.* The crucial dinner scene in the first book marks not harmony but the beginning of the division between the Tullivers and Dodsons. The reason seems to be that *The Mill on the Floss* concerns itself with people on "a lower level generally"—not "lower" in class but in the development of their moral perceptions—with a society not prepared for the higher sacrament. Indeed, it is likely that George Eliot sees Maggie's death by water as a preparation for the condition in which the society would be prepared.

Water, for Feuerbach, is the sacrament which symbolically asserts man's dependence on nature; the flood serves to remind man of this. Curiously, in water "the scales fall from [man's] eyes: he

25. "Preface" to the 1853 edition of his poems. Reprinted in *Mixed Essays, Irish Essays, and Others* (New York, 1883), p. 488.

26. An entry in her Journal for 12 Jan. 1859 records that "we went into town today and looked in the Annual Register for cases of *inundation*" (*The George Eliot Letters,* III, 33). The internal evidence that the flood was part of her conception from the first is sufficiently clear: the insistence on the Floss, the legend of St. Ogg, whose behavior foreshadows Maggie's, the constant allusions to past floods and future ones.

27. Knoepflmacher, pp. 307–309.

sees and thinks more clearly," and at the same time "human mental activity is nullified." [28] Both these effects of water operate in *The Mill on the Floss*. With Stephen Maggie falls into oblivion as she floats downstream; by contrast, with Tom the scales fall from her eyes as she reflects: "what quarrel, what harshness, what unbelief in each other can subsist in the presence of a great calamity, when all the artificial vesture of our life is gone, and we are all one with each other in primitive mortal needs" (Bk. vii, ch. v). Here, appropriately, Maggie not only "sees and thinks more clearly," but she is forced to these reflections by the power of Nature over the merely "artificial." And, of course, in the death which follows, consciousness is nullified, but only after, by symbolically crying "Maggie," Tom avers the love which dominated in the natural state of childhood. The death is a purification of both Maggie and Tom: "To purify oneself," as Feuerbach says, "to bathe, is the first, though the lowest of virtues." [29]

This, it seems to me, is George Eliot's attitude towards the final catastrophe; Tom and Maggie must achieve "the first, though the lowest of virtues" because even now neither they nor St. Ogg's is ready for the higher, active, creative virtues of man's full consciousness and power.

One more quotation from Feuerbach should suggest other ways in which the conclusion of *The Mill on the Floss* was firmly a part of the intellectual structure of the book: "It needs only that the ordinary course of things be interrupted in order to vindicate to common things an uncommon significance, *to life, as such, a religious import.* Therefore let bread be sacred for us, let wine be sacred, and also let water be sacred! Amen." For George Eliot, the inability to see the extraordinariness of the ordinary is an aspect of that egoism and lack of imagination which characterizes the society of St. Ogg's. She insists on the religious import, surely in Feuerbach's sense, of the ordinary, and thus follows Feuerbach by introducing into the novel the extraordinary—the flood—which is in fact only an extreme development of the ordinary and which in its extreme quality takes on the nature of a ritual. It is curious how so many of George Eliot's novels, however much the great bulk of events they

28. Feuerbach, p. 276.
29. Feuerbach, p. 275.

include are assertively ordinary, turn on events which seem to come directly out of melodrama—Arthur Donnithorne's last-minute rescue of Hetty, the final meeting of Baldassarre and Tito, Grandcourt's drowning and Mordecai's mystical Zionist visions, the revelation of Transome's relation to the lawer Jermyn.[30]

It is perhaps too simple to suggest that this sort of refusal to face the total implication of her own ideas and of her very temperament was the result of George Eliot's conscious effort to protect "her readers from any 'laming' effects."[31] Obviously George Eliot did seek moral order in the bleakest and most amoral elements of the world. But she was too intelligent to be satisfied with emotional need unsustained by intellectual conviction. Feuerbach, at least in *The Mill on the Floss,* seems to have supplied her with an intellectually satisfying and emotionally acceptable answer. Because we take George Eliot's perceptions to the point of the modern vision, where the only affirmation is personal, inward, and isolated, we tend to believe that in honesty she needed to do the same thing. But she turns away with characteristic Victorian strength and integrity in search of meaning, justice, and the organic community. We could do much worse.

30. See Barbara Hardy's discussion of the uses of coincidence in the novels in *The Novels of George Eliot* (London, 1959), esp. chs. vi and vii.
31. Allott, p. 106.

Felix Holt:
Society as Protagonist

by David R. Carroll

It is clear that by the time she wrote *Felix Holt* George Eliot
was becoming increasingly concerned in her novels with the relationship between the individual and society. This concern is not
merely that of any novelist who of necessity has to deal with the
contact between the central character and his immediate fellow
human beings. George Eliot envisages society in her novels not
only as an aggregation of individual relationships, but also as a
collective entity. She places this entity alongside the individual as
an actor in the drama and traces their interrelationship, insisting
upon their interdependence by means of the structure of her novels.

In *Romola* the political and religious developments of the society
had almost equal status with the private affairs of the individual.
George Eliot was there exploring the relationship between the individual and society by means of a parallel presentation of essentially the same problem on the plane of public events and the plane
of personal relationships. For most of the novel the two spheres of
action are separate, yet George Eliot sees the same fundamental
laws at work in each, and at the end she attempts to isolate their
essential, common morality. But there are clear signs in *Romola*
that George Eliot is becoming more and more aware of complexities inherent in her conception of the social organism. For example,
in the clash between Romola and Savonarola over the fate of

"*Felix Holt*: Society as Protagonist" by David R. Carroll. From *Nineteenth-
Century Fiction*, XVII, No. 3 (December, 1962), 237–52. Copyright © 1962 by
The Regents of the University of California. Reprinted by permission of the
author and The Regents.

Bernado, we see two characters looking at a problem from equally valid yet incompatible points of view; the dilemma occurs when, for the moment, macrocosm and microcosm are not merely juxtaposed for the sake of demonstrating the working of universal laws, but are shown in conflict. This conflict means in fact that the metaphor of the social organism has broken down. Man is a part of the social organism, but he is also a self-determining individual in contact with other self-determining individuals, and in *Romola* we have the suggestion that these two roles may be incompatible. It is this problem that is developed as the central theme in the last three novels, and that gives rise to a new structure most strikingly in *Felix Holt* and *Daniel Deronda*. In these novels, instead of placing a drama of personal relationships against a background of analogous political events, George Eliot uses as her central character someone fully involved in both worlds simultaneously. There was an anticipation of this structural innovation as early as "Janet's Repentance," where the Rev. Tryan attempts to reform simultaneously both Janet Dempster and the town of Milby. The emphasis in this early story is on the parallel regeneration of the individual and of the society rather than on Tryan's assimilation of his two roles, but the action does lead to one of George Eliot's most seminal generalizations which looks ahead to the later novels:

> Our subtlest analysis of schools and sects must miss the essential truth, unless it be lit up by the love that sees in all forms of human thought and work, the life and death struggles of separate human beings (x).[1]

This understanding of "schools and sects" and societies comes from one's own personal relationships. If one is not fully committed to these, any attempt to wider understanding or efficacy is impossible. George Eliot asserts this repeatedly in her last three novels by presenting the central character in the double role of private individual and public reformer, and showing how each is dependent on the other. Deronda's larger aims appear to be bedevilled by his relationship with Gwendolen until the end of the novel when it is precisely his contact with her supreme suffering that makes real for him the suffering of the Jews and precipitates him into his public role. No longer are the worlds of social and political action and

---

1. All references to quotations are by chapter.

that of the private individual merely juxtaposed—now they meet
and interact in the minds of the central characters.

At the center of *Felix Holt* is the titular hero engaged in a
private and public relationship. He is trying to reform both Esther
Lyon and the working class. He sees the two roles as being quite
separate and incompatible, and his development through the novel
is from his initial scorn of her and of women in general, as being
obstructive to his larger aims, to his final realization that his relationship with her is inseparable from those aims of social reform.
At the end of the novel, Felix achieves a more mature political
outlook simultaneously with his marriage to Esther. This development of the hero is worth looking at more closely, for, in company
with Deronda, Felix Holt is still seen by many critics as a static,
ideal character; and such a conception makes most of the novel
meaningless.

On his first appearance in the novel, Felix complacently diagnoses
his own fault of character to the Reverend Lyon:

> "I'm perhaps a little too fond of banging and smashing," he went on;
> "a phrenologist at Glasgow told me I had large veneration; another
> man there, who knew me, laughed out and said I was the most blas-
> phemous iconoclast living. 'That,' says my phrenologist, 'is because of
> his large Ideality, which prevents him from finding anything perfect
> enough to be venerated.' Of course, I put my ears down, and wagged
> my tail at that stroking" (v).

This iconoclasm, what Lyon later calls his "too confident self-
reliance" (xxxvii), is manifested both in Felix's relations with
Esther, and in his aims of social reform. To Esther, he says: "That's
what makes women a curse; all life is stunted to suit their little-
ness. That's why I'll never love, if I can help it; and if I love, I'll
bear it, and never marry" (x). This rejection of personal commitment on the assumption that it will conflict with his public task
is closely linked with his lack of realism in politics: "Felix Holt
had his illusions like other young men, though they were not of
a fashionable sort" (xi). His idealism is made dangerous by the
sudden rash fits of rebellion with which he springs to its defence.
And Lyon warns Felix against this failing: "You yourself are a
lover of freedom, and a bold rebel against usurping authority. But

the right to rebellion is the right to seek a higher rule, and not to wander in mere lawlessness" (xiii). These two aspects of his icono-clasm, the personal and the public, must be seen as symptoms of the same fault of character.

The interdependence of Felix's two roles is suggested structurally in a parallel series of events which contradicts his assertion of their incompatibility. Especially important is the election riot which occurs simultaneously with his rejection of Esther's love. The riot has already begun when Felix goes to Esther and renounces her love: "He felt that they must not marry—that they would ruin each other's lives. But he had longed for her to know fully that his will to be always apart from her was renunciation, not an easy preference" (xxxii). Immediately afterwards, he becomes involved in the riot, when, seeing his plans disintegrating, he over-confidently imagines he can control events: "He believed he had the power, and he was resolved to try, to carry the dangerous mass out of mischief till the military came to awe them" (xxxiii). While attempting this he inadvertently kills a man, and then the mob gets out of hand. His "too confident self-reliance" has caused the double failure.

Felix is imprisoned, Esther whisked off to Transome Court, and all appears to be lost. But she saves him from his double misfortune —publicly by speaking out for him in court and so inspiring the petition, privately by insisting on her love for him. It is then that Felix realizes that his two roles are not incompatible, that through her he can integrate the discrete halves of his life: "her woman's passion and her reverence for rarest goodness rushed together in an undivided current" (xlvi). Now that he has found something "perfect enough to be venerated" in his private relationships, there is a corresponding maturing of his political iconoclasm:

> "But I'm proof against that word failure. I've seen behind it. The only failure a man ought to fear is failure in cleaving to the purpose he sees to be best. As to just the amount of result he may see from his particular work—that's a tremendous uncertainty: the universe has not been arranged for the gratification of his feelings . . ." (xlv).

His love for Esther is inseparable from his political acknowledge-ment of the "higher rule" to which he is now prepared to conform.

George Eliot does not rely wholly on the parallelism of events to show the interdependence of the two halves of Felix's life. In order to insist that the "subtlest analysis of schools and sects" and societies must be illuminated by an understanding and awareness of "separate human beings," she draws an analogy between the development of Treby Magna and the development of Esther. Both macrocosm and microcosm obey similar laws of organic growth. George Eliot uses a similar device in *Middlemarch* where the detailed analogy between Dorothea's progress through the novel and the last few years of the Reform movement asserts that she embodies in her strivings the essence of reform; so, when Ladislaw comes to love and understand Dorothea, he is enabled to participate effectively in the larger movement she epitomizes. Analogy is used for the same purpose here.

Esther, living at Treby, frustrated in her desires for social advancement, comes under the influence of Felix Holt who shatters her genteel ideas. Her horizons expand and she begins to feel "that if Felix Holt were to love her, her life would be exalted into something quite new—into a sort of difficult blessedness, such as one may imagine in beings who are conscious of painfully growing into the possession of higher powers" (xxii). She sees him as the means of "checking her self-satisfied pettiness with the suggestion of a wider life" (xxxvii). But Felix's influence is removed when Esther, discovering the facts of her past, is taken to Transome Court for a rehearsal of her new position in society. Here, under the influence of Harold Transome, she begins to leave "the high mountain air" of Felix's love, and to "adjust her wishes to a life of middling delights" (xliv). Thanks, however, to the continued influence of Felix, she comes to see through the gentility of Transome Court, rejects Harold, and returns to Felix. If we juxtapose this sequence of events with the description in the third chapter of the political development of Treby Magna, it is clear that an analogy is implied. Just as for Esther the main concern of her life "was not religious differences, but social differences" (vi), so Treby society was mainly interested in social position—the Debarrys "as lords of the manor, naturally came next to Providence and took the place of the saints" (iii). Treby Magna remained in this state of narrow-minded complacency "until there befell new conditions, complicating its relation with the rest of the world, and gradually awakening in it that higher consciousness which is known to bring higher pains" (iii). These new conditions are the canal and the coal mines breaking down the isolation of Treby; but thirdly there is the attempt to check this movement, to prevent the merging of Treby with the expanding industrial development of the country by the discovery and exploitation of "a saline spring, which suggested to a too constructive brain the possibility of turning Treby Magna into a fashionable watering-place" (iii). Jermyn carries the plan through and the town discovers the facts of its past: "an excellent guide-book and descriptive cards surmounted by vignettes were printed and Treby Magna became conscious of certain facts in its own history of which it had previously been in contented ignorance" (iii). Each sojourn in the higher strata of society is short-lived: Esther returns to Felix and the working-class, while "The Spa, for some mysterious reason, did not succeed" (iii). The town reassumes its initial movement toward integration into the national, industrial economy:

> In this way it happened that Treby Magna gradually passed from being simply a respectable market-town . . . and took on the more complex life brought by mines and manufactures, which belong more directly to the great circulating system of the nation than to the local system to which they have been superadded . . . (iii).[2]

When this analogy between the development of Esther and Treby is understood, the generalization that closes the political biography of the town comes to have a greatly increased significance:

> These social changes in Treby parish are comparatively public· matters, and this history is chiefly concerned with the private lot of a few men and women; but there is no private life which has not been determined by a wider public life, from the time when the primeval milkmaid had to wander with the wanderings of her clan, because the cow she milked was one of a herd which had made the pasture bare (iii).

We can see now that this generalization elucidates the analogy we have just examined and the central structure of the novel. The same laws are operating in both the development of Esther and

---

2. It is interesting to notice that the forces, principally those of commerce and manufacture, which in *The Mill on the Floss* were seen as fatal to the roots of society, are here seen as necessary forces of integration.

of Treby, and so the attempt of Felix to separate his public task of reform from his private relationship with Esther is impossible, and fatal to his political understanding.

The intimate connection between the two halves of Felix's life is again insisted on by a common religious imagery and terminology. He envisages his political task persistently in religious terms. For example, he tells Lyon that he "was converted by six weeks' debauchery" (v) to his present political creed; also, he has a political "congregation" (v) which he addresses weekly in the same room where Lyon holds his Wednesday preachings (xi). He finds support for his sections from St. Paul (v) and the "old Catholics" (xxvii), and at his trial asserts one of the articles of his creed in suitably religious terms:

> "I hold it blasphemy to say that a man ought not to fight against authority: there is no great religion and no great freedom that has not done it, in the beginning . . . I should hold myself the worst sort of traitor if I put my hand either to fighting or disorder . . . if I were not urged to it by what I hold to be sacred feelings, making a sacred duty either to my own manhood or to my fellow-man" (xlvi).

And during the election when he addresses the working-men we see that he has appropriated not only a terminology but also a ritual: "he stepped on to the stone, and took off his cap by an instinctive prompting that always led him to speak uncovered" (xxx).

A complementary series of images is used to describe the personal relationship between Felix and Esther, from the latter's point of view. For example, after Felix has renounced her love, Esther's sentiments become religiose; she

> . . . began to look on all that had passed between herself and Felix as something not buried, but embalmed and kept as a relic in a private sanctuary. . . . The best part of a woman's love is worship; but it is hard to be sent away with her precious spikenard rejected, and her long tresses too, that were let fall ready to soothe the wearied feet (xxxvii).

Similarly, at the end of the novel, the renovation of her life from "a heap of fragments" (xv) is expressed in an extended religious image.

It is only in that freshness of our time that the choice is possible which gives unity to life, and makes the memory a temple where all relics and all votive offerings, all worship, and all grateful joy, are an unbroken history sanctified by one religion (xliv).

The insistently religious nature of these two strands of imagery is constantly trying to bring together the two halves of Felix's life which they describe. He is equally insistent on their incompatibility.

George Eliot's use of religious imagery is one of the most striking and pervasive features of *Felix Holt*. An awareness of it leads us straight to the central and most recurrent theme of the novel. This is the belief in the necessity for everyone to embrace a "religion"—and the concomitants of what a religion means for George Eliot are clearly enumerated in one of the phases of Esther's regeneration:

Esther had been so long used to hear the formulas of her father's belief without feeling or understanding them that they had lost all power to touch her. The first religious experience of her life—the first self-questioning, the first voluntary subjection, the first longing to acquire the strength of greater motives and obey the more strenuous rule—had come to her through Felix Holt (xxvii).

It is in this context that we can understand the importance of Lyon and the reason for his ambivalent presentation. He plays an important part in the novel, influencing both Felix and Esther because he stands as the type of the person who has submitted himself to "the more strenuous rule," and his eccentricities of dress, speech, and behavior all spring from this. The reason for his importance is to be found not in his sectarian noncomformity, which is rejected by the main characters, but in his past. It is this which sanctions his utterances. While a highly successful minister, he had fallen in love with Esther's mother, "an unregenerate Catholic," and his public role had to be forsaken: "A terrible crisis had come upon him; a moment in which religious doubt and newly-awakened passion had rushed together in common flood, and had paralysed his ministerial gifts" (vi). This is a preenactment of Felix's fear of personal involvement with Esther. Lyon abandons the ministry and devotes himself to Annette, but it is this contact with what our opening generalization called "the life and death struggles of separate human beings" which brings him real knowledge:

> Strange! that the passion for this woman, which he felt to have drawn him aside from the right as much as if he had broken the most solemn vows . . . the passion for a being who had no glimpse of his thoughts induced a more thorough renunciation than he had ever known in the time of his complete devotion to his ministerial career (vi).

Just as Felix modifies his political aims on accepting Esther's love, so Lyon on returning to the ministry after Annette's death began to extend his idea of "the limits of salvation, which he had in one sermon even hinted might extend to unconscious recipients of mercy" (vi). Clearly this flashback into Lyon's past occurring early in the novel is a preliminary statement of the main theme, supporting Felix's fears at the same time as it challenges Esther's love: can she, unlike her mother who while living with Lyon "regarded her present life as a sort of death to the world" (vi) help to unify Felix's life?

This redefinition of religion through the presentation of Lyon's character is an important evaluative element in the novel. His presence sanctions, as it were, the use of religious terminology for a wide range of experiences, in particular Esther's love and Felix's social aims. We have already seen Esther enumerating the articles of her drastically demythologized religion of love for Felix, and the latter seeing his politics as a religious crusade. In addition, George Eliot draws some detailed analogies between Lyon's religious and Felix's political utterances. For example, Lyon's preparatory sermon:

> "My brethren, do you think that great shout was raised in Israel by each man's waiting to say 'amen' till his neighbours had said 'amen'? Do you think there will ever be a great shout for the right—the shout of a nation as of one man, rounded and whole, like the voice of the archangel that bound together all the listeners of earth and heaven— if every Christian of you peeps round to see what his neighbours in good coats are doing . . . ?" (iv).

expresses the same sentiments as Felix's secular sermon to the working-men:

"I'll tell you what's the greatest power under heaven," said Felix, "and that is public opinion—the ruling belief in society about what is right and what is wrong, what is honourable and what is shameful. . . . How can political freedom make us better, any more than a religion we don't believe in, if people laugh and wink when they see men abuse and defile it? And while public opinion is what it is . . . no fresh scheme of voting will much mend our condition" (xxx).

In the same way, Lyon's remarks on the function of his choir are clearly a political comment directed at the exclusive world of Transome Court or perhaps at the exclusive electorate of the First Reform Act:

". . . we must be content to carry a thorn in our sides while the necessities of our imperfect state demand that there should be a body set apart and called a choir, whose special office it is to lead the singing, not because they are more disposed to the devout uplifting of praise, but because they are endowed with better vocal organs, and have attained more of the musician's art. For all office, unless it be accompanied by peculiar grace, becomes, as it were, a diseased organ, seeking to make itself too much of a centre. Singers, specially so called, are, it must be confessed, an anomaly among us who seek to reduce the Church to its primitive simplicity and to cast away all that may obstruct the direct communion of spirit with spirit" (xiii).

After the unregenerate Felix has suggested that it is "a denial of private judgment" to make everyone sing the same tune, he is corrected by Lyon who proceeds to generalize the discussion:

"You yourself are a lover of freedom, and a bold rebel against usurping authority. But the right of rebellion is the right to seek a higher rule, and not to wander in mere lawlessness. . . . And I apprehend . . . that there is a law in music, disobedience whereunto would bring us in our singing to the level of shrieking maniacs or howling beasts: so that herein we are well instructed how true liberty can be nought but the transfer of obedience from the will of one or of a few men to that will which is the norm or rule for all men . . . (xiii).

Such analogies help to generalize the central theme through apparently self-contained sections of the novel. The transcription of Esther's and Felix's aspirations and beliefs into Lyon's terminology is also a means of evaluation: how do they stand up to the shift into the vocabulary of someone who sees all things *sub specie aeternitatis*? " 'Why not Wellington as well as Rabshakeh? and why not Brougham as well as Balaam?' " (v), asks Lyon. This constant interplay of analogy between the spheres of love, politics, and religion, is one of the most sustained devices in *Felix Holt*, anticipating the equally important role it plays in George Eliot's last two novels.

Once the basic structure of the novel and the full importance of Lyon have been grasped, the contrasted world of Transome Court fits significantly into the design. Harold Transome reinforces the structure: he too is engaged in the double role of politician and lover, in each of which he opposes Felix. Felix's political hopes are shattered in the riot instigated by Harold's agents, while at Transome Court Harold attempts to counter the regenerating influence he has had on Esther. And yet the two men have a great deal in common. Just as Felix's political iconoclasm was shown to be another facet of his scorn of Esther, so Harold's bogus Radicalism is revealed in its true light by his personal relationships—particularly with women. The irony of the fact that his first wife was a slave escapes him, but not Esther, who while at Transome Court comes to understand the complementary nature of his political and private lives:

> His very good-nature was unsympathetic: it never came from any thorough understanding or deep respect for what was in the mind of the person he obliged or indulged; it was like his kindness to his mother—an arrangement of his for the happiness of others, which, if they were sensible, ought to succeed. And an inevitable comparison which haunted her, showed her the same quality in his political views: the utmost enjoyment of his own advantages was the solvent that blended pride in his family and position, with the adhesion to changes that were to obliterate tradition and melt down enchased gold heirlooms into plating for ᵗhe egg-spoons of "the people" (xliii).

This interpenetration of the politician and the private individual, both in the case of Harold and of Felix, is not only described, it is enacted dramatically with searching irony. In the conversations the two men have with Esther, we see politics being used as a precise expression of character.

Harold, like Felix, has a "too confident self-reliance," but whereas the latter's is directed towards an altruistic object, Harold's is egoistic.[3] His failure and punishment are correspondingly more severe, and only at the end of the novel is there a suggestion of regeneration. Once again Lyon is used as the means of assessing the values of the central characters. A powerful effect is obtained by the juxtaposition of the practical man of business who is unwittingly bringing about his own downfall, and the eccentric, other-worldly Lyon; the author's comment further defines the central theme of the novel:

> . . . but I never smiled at Mr Lyon's trustful energy without falling to penitence and veneration immediately after. For what we call illusions are often, in truth, a wider vision of past and present realities—a willing movement of a man's soul with the larger sweep of the world's forces—a movement towards a more assured end than the chances of a single life. . . .
>
> At present, looking back on that day at Treby, it seems to me that the sadder illusion lay with Harold Transome, who was trusting in his own skill to shape the success of his own morrows, ignorant of what many yesterdays had determined for him beforehand (xvi).

Just as Felix's punishment for "trusting in his own skill" too exclusively is the chaos of the election riot, so Harold comes to a full realization of his dependence upon others through the denouement of "the labyrinthine confusions of right and possession" (xliii) of the Transome Court theme.[4]

So far we have concentrated on that part of the novel in which the chief concern is the submission of self in the search for "a wider vision of past and present realities." In startling contrast to this is the somber world of Transome Court where the self is all-important and the chief concern is the despairing attempt to escape from these same "realities." In this world, Mrs. Transome stands, in stark antithesis to Lyon, as the type of "the clever sinner" (i), and her past must be contrasted with his. The clash between Lyon's religious beliefs and his personal experiences led to a mature and tolerant

3. A caricature of Harold's political beliefs is the publican Chubb's "political 'idee', which was, that society existed for the sake of the individual, and that the name of that individual was Chubb" (xi).

4. One is the "confusions of right and possession" at the level of personal intrigue, the other at the level of party politics.

philosophy; there is a similar clash in Mrs. Transome's life, but here there is no reconciliation. Her creed is simple:

> She had no ultimate analysis of things that went beyond blood and family—the Herons of Fenshore or the Badgers of Hillbury. She had never seen behind the canvas with which her life was hung. In the dim background there was the burning mount and the tables of the law; in the foreground there was Lady Debarry privately gossiping about her . . . (xl).

In "fatal inconsistency" with this creed of "blood and family" is her past adultery with Jermyn; they "had seen no reason why they should not indulge their passion and their vanity, and determine for themselves how their lives should be made delightful in spite of unalterable external conditions" (xxi). The presentation of the faded Mrs. Transome at Transome Court still living by the creed she has defiled is without doubt one of George Eliot's supreme achievements. The tragedy of her position is conveyed initially without explicit comment on her past, and our awareness develops through dramatic hints and juxtapositions until everything is suddenly made clear.

The actual moment of revelation comes, I think, in chapter viii, and it provides an excellent example of George Eliot's method. Most of the chapter is taken up with a discussion of Harold's character, particularly his brash egoism, and with his mother's unexplained fears at his treatment of Jermyn. We do not know at this point in the novel why she is so apprehensive of her son's reforms, why "she trembled under his kindness." The chapter ends with this superbly restrained yet ominous paragraph which is a foretaste of the somber and tense world of *Daniel Deronda*:

> She was standing on the broad gravel in the afternoon; the long shadows lay on the grass; the light seemed the more glorious because of the reddened and golden trees. The gardeners were busy at their pleasant work; the newly-turned soil gave out an agreeable fragrance; and little Harry was playing with Nimrod round old Mr Transome, who sat placidly on a low garden-chair. The scene would have made a charming picture of English domestic life, and the handsome, majestic, grey-haired woman (obviously grandmamma) would have been especially admired. But the artist would have felt it requisite to turn her face towards her husband and little grandson, and to have given

her an elderly amiability of expression which would have divided
remark with his exquisite rendering of her Indian shawl. Mrs Transome's face was turned the other way, and for this reason she only
heard an approaching step, and did not see whose it was; yet it startled
her: it was not quick enough to be her son's step, and besides, Harold
was away at Duffield. It was Mr Jermyn's.

Jermyn's approach explains silently and dramatically the lapse
from the conventional in the "charming picture of English domestic life" at Transome Court; he comes to provide the missing factor
in the picture and to explain Mrs. Transome's lack of "an elderly
amiability of expression." Then, in this role, he is linked significantly with Harold by the startled Mrs. Transome, who is fully
aware of the difference in their steps. These hints bridge the emotional gap between the apparent unimportance of Jermyn's arrival
and the tension with which it is described, and suddenly the true
relationship of the three characters becomes perfectly clear. Without
any explicit comment the secret of Mrs. Transome's dilemma is
revealed. And alongside our awareness of this is plotted with ap-
palling irony the increasing assertiveness of Harold's egoistic will.

This is not the "willing movement of a man's soul with the
larger sweep of the world's forces," but an attempt by the three
protagonists to escape from these forces now turned Nemesis.
George Eliot is showing us here the reverse of her familiar theme
of the search for a social ethic; Esther is liberated by the vision of
"a wider life" (xxxvii), while Harold is punished by the shattering
revelation of his sonship when he feels for the first time "the hard
pressure of our common lot, the yoke of that mighty resistless
destiny laid upon us by the acts of other men as well as our own"
(xlix). The function of the extremely complex plot is clearly to
demonstrate dramatically this close interconnection between the
members of society.

The contrast between Mrs. Transome and Lyon must be insisted
on. When his past returns to threaten him, he acts typically in
persevering with the religious debate:

> What if he were inwardly torn by doubt and anxiety concerning his
> own private relations and the facts of his own past life? That danger
> of absorption within the narrow bounds of self only urged him the
> more towards action which had a wider bearing, and might tell on
> the welfare of England at large (xv).

As the revelation of Mrs. Transome's past approaches, she shrinks closer and closer within herself:

> Here she moved to and fro among the rose coloured satin of chairs and curtains—the great story of the world reduced for her to the little tale of her own existence—dull obscurity everywhere, except where the keen light fell on the narrow track of her own lot, wide only for a woman's anguish (xxxiv).

To describe this moral response, images of sacrilege replace the religious imagery of the other half of the novel. The full awareness of this contrast is brought home to us with the sudden introduction of Esther to Transome Court. Up to this point in the novel, she has been alternately annoyed and impressed by the high ideals of Felix and her father; now she moves into the isolated, darker world of Transome Court where such ideals are unknown. The two sides of her character come into equal conflict: the unregenerate Esther, a Mrs. Transome in embryo, is attracted by the genteelness of Transome Court and the homage paid her by Harold, while the partly reformed Esther gradually becomes aware of the hollowness of this existence and "the threadbare tissue of this majestic lady's life" (xlix). The question is, will she succumb to its "middling delights, overhung with the langourous haziness of motiveless ease" (xliv), before she comes to realize the full relevance of the "desecrated sanctities" of Mrs. Transome's life, to her own future? As we have seen, this is a quest for a "religion" and Esther is led to her final choice by two "visions." The first was the revelation of Lyon's past, "a vision of passion and struggle, of delight and renunciation" (xxvi) which epitomizes one ethic of the novel. This is followed by the "vision of consequences" (xxxviii), the sight of Mrs. Transome at her moment of supreme suffering:

> The dimly-suggested tragedy of this woman's life, the dreary waste of years empty of sweet trust and affection, afflicted her even to horror. It seemed to have come as a last vision to urge her towards the life where the draughts of joy sprang from the unchanging fountains of reverence and devout love (l).

Now she sees the full relevance of Mrs. Transome's past to her own relationship with Harold, and so she turns instinctively to Felix.

Esther's choice is not merely a personal choice of Felix but also a social commitment to the working-class. This aspect is underlined by the parallel with the biblical Esther. Even before her elevation of rank, she is seen "in this small dingy house of the minister in Malthouse Yard" as "a light-footed, sweet-voiced Queen Esther" (vi). Later at Transome Court, Harold assures her that she is "empress" of her fortune, even though she confesses "I don't think I know very well what to do with my empire" (xl). As might be expected, the biblical parallel is further developed by Lyon, who looks at everything from the same panoramic point of view: "he was so accustomed to the impersonal study of narrative, that even in these exceptional moments the habit of half a century asserted itself, and he seemed sometimes not to distinguish the case of Esther's inheritance from a story in ancient history" (xxxviii). For the Jews he substitutes the "body of congregational Dissent," and hopes Esther will fulfill her ordained role " 'Your education and peculiar history would thus be seen to have coincided with a long train of events in making this family property a means of honouring and illustrating a purer form of Christianity than that which hath unhappily obtained the pre-eminence in this land' " (xli). His interpretation is wrong, but Esther does continue her biblical role at the trial when she uses her new position to appeal for Felix, identifying herself with the people among whom she has been brought up: "Some of that ardour which has flashed out and illuminated all poetry and history was burning today in the bosom of sweet Esther Lyon" (xlvi). The two aspects of her choice must be given equal importance if we are to understand how she is the woman who can make "a man's passion for her rush in one current with all the great aims of his life" (xxvii).

Indeed, the almost complete concentration of interest upon Esther in the last third of the novel is responsible for the final lack of balance. The titular hero waits passively in prison for the regeneration of Esther to be completed so that his divided life can be unified. Poised between the contrasting worlds of the novel, she is given the final task of evaluation, and it is an anticlimax to realize at the end that as a reward for her rejection of the world of Transome Court she is allowed to marry Felix, who has throughout been insulated from its corroding gentility. In fact, she has usurped Felix's central position, so obscuring the nature of his education. George Eliot solves a similar structural problem much more satisfactorily in *Daniel Deronda*, where Deronda remains throughout delicately poised between the Jews and Gwendolen, who at the end combine to effect a complete integration of his character. But it is significant that in order to achieve this finer balance George Eliot has to share Esther's role between Gwendolen and Mirah.

Felix Holt is, then, a novel about the organic nature of society. The themes of politics, religion and love, all demonstrate that neither the claims of the microcosm nor of the macrocosm can be neglected. Any attempt to reform or modify the social organism without due regard for, and commitment to, the individual is bound to fail from lack of reality, just as an egoistic assertion of the claims of the individual will fail by its very exclusiveness. The difficulties of the search for a social ethic are defined in all of George Eliot's novels, but here she is grappling openly with the complications and contradictions inherent in the very idea of a social ethic, in the very conception of the social organism. Perhaps there is an indication of her increasing awareness of these difficulties in the remarkable conviction with which in this novel she reverses this favorite theme of the search for an ethic and depicts a whole world in which society is seen as Nemesis pursuing and punishing those individuals who refuse its claims. One is the theme of worship and high endeavor, the other of sacrilege and punishment. The god in each case is society.

George Eliot in *Middlemarch*

by Quentin Anderson

In *The Prelude* Wordsworth notes that while he was taken up
with Godwinian rationalism he had discovered that rationalism had
a special danger: it denied the existence of the passions which actually informed it. The briefest possible answer to the question,
What is the greatness of George Eliot? is to say that she knew and
could show that every idea is attended by a passion; that thought
is a passional act. Of course it is on the showing, the accomplishment
of the artist, that the emphasis must finally rest, but it seems politic
to begin this account by suggesting to a somewhat unreceptive age
how much she has to tell her readers. Widely read and highly
respected during the last four decades of her century, George Eliot
(1819–80) became schoolroom fare in ours. But the assumption that
she is once more coming into the light, if current, may be the misleading consequence of the appearance of Professor Gordon Haight's
monumental edition of her *Letters* and F. R. Leavis's fine chapters
on her in *The Great Tradition*. There is a seeming paradox in the
fact that, although admired, she is not much read, because no novelist in English has come closer to answering a question which is very
important to us: How can a social world be felt and understood? It
appears probable that there is some resistance in us against the
terms in which George Eliot answers this question; we may well
want a chance for vicarious or imagined mastery over the social
order—a chance to judge and discriminate with sureness—but most
of us find something remote, something truly "Victorian," in a
world so fully humanized as the world of *Middlemarch;* perhaps

"George Eliot in *Middlemarch*" by Quentin Anderson. From *The Pelican
Guide to English Literature*, Vol. 6, *From Dickens to Hardy*, ed. Boris Ford,
1958 (London and New York: Penguin Books, rev. ed., 1966), 274–93. Copyright
© Penguin Books Ltd. 1958. Reprinted by permission of the publisher.

this is because it requires more love than we can give, more assurance than we can muster. Before we inquire just what *Middlemarch* does demand of us, a brief introduction is necessary.

George Eliot's Midland birth and lasting absorption in Midland scenes and manners largely defined her first efforts in fiction. The earnest, plain girl who kept house for her father, Robert Evans (her own given name was Mary Anne), was awkwardly and heavily pious in the way that girls who have no other way to express intense emotions are pious. Friendship with two families, the Brays and Hennells, who might be described as provincial intellectuals, widened her horizon immensely. She soon outstripped her friends, though she remained characteristically loyal to them, and became an enormous reader. Her first sustained literary endeavour was the translation of Strauss's *Das Leben Jesu* (1846), a work to which she was drawn by her earnest concern with the human meaning of the Christian legend, for legend it had now come to be for her. She made the leap from provincial society to the world of literature and ideas in London as assistant editor of the *Westminster Review*, which John Chapman was trying to put on its feet. She did some further translating (including Spinoza's *Ethics*), and, as a reviewer, formulated her requirements for fiction with prophetic precision. She did not undertake fiction herself until after she had made the great passional commitment of her life—to live as wife to George Henry Lewes, the gifted biographer, translator, and historian of philosophy. Since Lewes's wife was still living, the couple was socially stigmatized until the novelist won them a partial acceptance. Lewes's unremitting devotion and faith in her powers were essential to George Eliot. Their union covered the span of her productive life in fiction, which began with *Scenes of Clerical Life* in *Blackwood's* (1857).

Her second venture was *Adam Bede* (1859). This was followed by *The Mill on the Floss* (1860), *Silas Marner* (1861), *Romola* (in the *Cornhill*, 1862-3), *Felix Holt, the Radical* (1866), a dramatic poem, *The Spanish Gypsy* (1868), *Middlemarch* (which appeared in eight parts, 1871-2), and *Daniel Deronda* (1876). The works she published before *Romola*, an historical novel about Savonarola's Florence, all depend for their matter on her memories of childhood and young womanhood in Warwickshire, where eighteenth-century ways were still common in her day. *Adam Bede* and *The Mill on the Floss* remain delightful for their provincial humours and their affectionate rendering of a provincial scene; there are passages in both which are masterly, yet both at crucial moments demand that uncritical assent to affirmed rather than established motivations which the Victorian reader was so often ready to supply, partly because they were (or were supposed to be) his own, but more often perhaps simply because they were the condition of further vicarious participation in the feelings of an Adam Bede or a Maggie Tulliver. To find George Eliot at her best one turns to the three books which follow *Romola*. Among these, *Felix Holt, the Radical,* is much the weakest, though it contains superlative passages. *Daniel Deronda* is about the most splendid failure among English novels, and the reader who responds to *Middlemarch* may be assured that it is well worth his time. But *Middlemarch* is unquestionably the best of the three.

This novel is subtitled "A Study of Provincial Life," and the climax in the national life which it partly chronicles, the period in which the Reform Bill of 1832 was moving towards adoption, was selected with the apparent intention of giving the novel the representative quality which we associate with Flaubert's *Sentimental Education* and Tolstoy's *War and Peace.* But one of the first things we must note about the novel is that this particular intention masks a more general one. Flaubert's choice of the revolution of 1848 or Tolstoy's of Napoleon's invasion of Russia as events which bring together various strands of the national experience was motivated in part by a desire to put that experience before us. George Eliot's notebook for the novel shows that she looked up such matters as the stages in the passage of the Reform Bill, the medical horizons of the 1830s, the industrial uses of manganese, and various other details. But the uses to which she puts these things are not terminal; she is not concerned as Flaubert is to lodge firmly in the reader's sensibility a mass of impressions deliberately selected to inform us of the political, industrial, and social life of the time. She is, in fact, incapable of suggesting the tone of a given period or historical moment. In the Middlemarch world, as in George Eliot generally, change is something intrusive, an irruption from without. The more general intention of which I have spoken is the attempt to render in a novel her sense of the "primitive tissue" of a community.

This term is employed by Tertius Lydgate, a surgeon with excel-

lent training, who buys a Middlemarch practice and hopes to combine medical work with research in physiology. His studies in Paris
have persuaded him that a promising line of inquiry lies in the
attempt to find the primal tissue which is the basis of all those
adapted to special bodily functions. The master image of the book
precisely parallels Lydgate's physiological inquiry: this is the image
of human relationships as a web. Each of us stands at what seems to
us a centre, our own consciousness, though it is in fact but one of
numerous nodes or junction points. This is further illustrated in
George Eliot's figure of the metal mirror bearing many scratches,
which when illuminated at any given point produces the illusion of
concentric circles ranged about that point. This figure enriches the
suggestion of the recurrent web image and those associated with it by
enforcing the fact that in dealing with a particular person we must
consider: his appearance in the eyes of each of the other persons
whom he encounters; the way he appears among various social
groups to which he is known or which know of him; and his own
complex of feelings which leads him to offer the world a version (or
various versions) of himself. This does not at first seem an epoch-
making kind of viewpoint for a novelist, since all novelists must
somehow convey the quality of each character's self-regard and the
opinions that others have of him. But George Eliot's special success
in *Middlemarch* is the consequence of making the reciprocal work-
ings of self-regard and opinion primary—in effect an extraordinary
economy of means, and not simply of means, for it appears when we
look closely that the matter of the book is people's opinions about
one another, and that its particular method consists in contriving
scenes in which the disparity between the intentions of agents and
the opinions of observers is dramatically exhibited. This consistency
of method accounts for our sense of the unity of a book which embraces a whole social order and four, or by another reckoning, five
principal stories.

Of course these stories are intertwined by the plot as well as by
our developing sense of Middlemarch as a community. The first of
these stories is that of Dorothea Brooke, which was begun as an independent tale and later worked into the plan of the larger novel.
Dorothea is somewhat externally characterized in a brief "Prelude."
She belongs to a group of great spirits who remain unknown and

unsung: "with dim lights and tangled circumstance they tried to shape their thought and deed in noble agreement; but, after all, to common eyes their struggles seemed mere inconsistency and form-lessness; for these later-born Theresas were helped by no coherent social faith and order which could perform the function of knowl-edge for the ardently willing soul." The account concludes: "Here and there is born a Saint Theresa, foundress of nothing, whose loving heart-beats and sobs after an unattained goodness tremble off and are dispersed among hindrances, instead of centring in some long-recognizable deed." F. R. Leavis discerns a tendency on the part of George Eliot to make rather too personal investments in her heroines, and the tone of this "Prelude" bears him out. The reader ought to be assured that the Dorothea he meets in the opening scenes of the novel is not this portentous figure, but a young lady whose foible in marrying an elderly pedant has the consequences—comic, pathetic, and even, in a minor and domestic key, tragic—that we might expect it to have in life. As the novel goes forward, however, Dorothea's demand that the world afford chances for heroic achievement does begin to seem much too categorical. We must return to the question of her role in the imaginative economy of the novel at a later point.

Lydgate, the principal figure of the second intrigue, is closer to the working centre of the book than Dorothea, since his fate turns not simply on his marriage to Rosamond Vincy, but upon the sum of his actions and reactions in response to Middlemarch. His story is linked with the third in the group of four, the story of Bulstrode, the banker guilty of moral defalcations, whose self-arraignment is one of the finest episodes in the book (although the whole Bulstrode strand in the novel is less impressive than the others because his past is somewhat stagily rendered and the agents out of that past who hunt him down seem melodramatic conveniences). The fourth strand, closer in tone to the earlier Midland novels, functions in part to provide a standard by which the others may be placed and judged. It involves the Garth family, Mary, her father, Caleb, her successful suitor Fred Vincy, and the Reverend Farebrother, who also aspires to Mary. Here also belong the provincial humours of the book, which centre about old Peter Featherstone's disposition of his property.

Middlemarch is carefully (contemporary readers tend to say exhaustively) plotted. One or more of the characters in each of the four stories plays an important part in each of the other three. The Victorian reader was offered a multiplicity of occasions for sympathetic concern. One of the things about George Eliot and her readers which it is hardest for us to recapture is the artless and unashamed emotionalism of the latter over the fate of her characters, and the benign acceptance of this situation on the part of the writer. The century which wrenched Hamlet out of *Hamlet* had not the least scruple about lobbying for its favourite character while the novel was in the course of publication in parts—while it was in fact still being written. One may imagine that if the modern objection to such innocence about the fashion in which a work is made an artistic whole had been stated it would have been met with the response that the whole was really constituted by the assurance of moral conformity—George Eliot could be trusted. Blackwood, George Eliot's publisher, wrote her in this vein while *Middlemarch* was appearing; he sets down his hopes and fears for the characters, and tells her in effect that her interposition in their lives has been both touching and morally impeccable. The novelist and her fellows were of course affected by this atmosphere: they wrote with a consciousness of the awakened and palpitant sensibilities of the readers who were speculating about what would happen in the next part; they watched the sale of each part with anxiety, and made anxious inquiry about a falling-off. Some of the occasions for sympathetic concern in this novel may be listed: How will Dorothea awake to a consciousness of the meaning of her marriage to the pedant, Casaubon? Will Fred Vincy inherit old Featherstone's money? Failing that, will he reclaim himself and marry Mary Garth, or will Farebrother cut him out? Will Rosamond's "torpedo contact" paralyse her vigorous husband, Lydgate? Can he succeed in medical practice in the face of the bigotry of Middlemarch? Can he extricate himself from his debts? How will Bulstrode be found out, and what will thereupon happen to him and his devoted wife? There is a cognate familiarity about many of the motifs of the story: the idealism of Dorothea, the earnest and rather wry Christianity of Farebrother, the weakling reclaimed in Fred Vincy, the dryness, harsh fun, and moral beauty of the plain Mary Garth. Neither plot nor traits of character taken alone are sufficiently distinctive to set this novel apart from others. I have found that youthful readers nowadays are restive when confronted by such careful plotting and such familiar traits of character; they shy away and quite miss the light which illumines all these things in their mutual relations, the voice of the wise woman. That voice is often heard speaking directly with an authority which makes use of the Victorian reader's involvement with the characters to make him look up and look about, to see how human relations are established within the world of the story—to see the whole of what the wise woman surveys.

What she surveys may be called a landscape of opinion, for it is not the natural landscape that is dominant here. In fact, there are only two fully realized natural landscapes, Lowick Manor and Stone Court, and in these cases the landscape is realized by an individual whose situation and interests make him aware of an external world at that particular moment. For the most part we may characterize the book's use of the physical world by referring to George Eliot's own sense of Warwickshire as a physical locale which has been wholly humanized, and to the Reverend Cadwallader's half-serious remark that it is a very good quality in a man to have a trout stream. This transposition of the natural into the moral and psychological is further illustrated by the novelist's use of snatches of poetry— Dorothea Brooke's hope for social betterment "haunted her like a passion"—and we may say that the affectionate sense of nature and the objects that man makes and handles which suffuses *Adam Bede* has been deliberately subdued here. Nothing comparable to the description of Hetty Sorrel in Mrs. Poyser's dairy can enter into *Middlemarch,* not because it is a more "intellectual" book, but because its immediacies are not things seen but things felt and believed. It is striking that we know almost nothing of the appearance of Middlemarch itself, although our sense of the life of the town as a community is very full indeed, ranging as it does from a pot-house to the Green Dragon, the town's best inn, from horse-dealers, auctioneers, and grocers to the lawyers, physicians, merchants, clergymen, and landowners who stand at the head of the scale. Although we see little of the activities of all these people we hear their voices, each pitched to the tone of its own desire, each capable of dropping suggestively or rising assertively on grounds which George

Eliot shows to be wholly inadequate when related to the facts of the particular case. Chapter 45 is a good instance of the masterly way in which she can demonstrate the drifts and swirls of opinion through the town. In this account of various responses to Lydgate's principled refusal to dispense drugs himself, each of the voices establishes a character so fully and with such economy that it is hard to believe that Mawmsey, the grocer, and Mrs. Dollop of the Tankard have not always been known to us. Yet this single chapter does much more. In it we learn that the clouds of misapprehension and selfishness gathering about Lydgate cannot possibly be dispelled, that he is more than likely to get into debt, and that his wife's awful insularity will resist his earnest and even his desperate attempts to penetrate it. George Eliot had much earlier (Chapter 15) used her author's privilege to warn the reader of all these possibilities. "For surely all must admit that a man may be puffed and belauded, envied, ridiculed, counted upon as a tool and fallen in love with, or at least selected as a future husband, and yet remain virtually unknown—known merely as a cluster of signs for his neighbours' false suppositions." The novelist, writing of *Middlemarch,* says: "I wanted to give a panoramic view of provincial life . . . ," but what she does give is something far more active, far more in accord with the image of the web—or of a vast switchboard in which every signal is interpreted differently by each receiver, and each receiver is in its turn capable of propagating in response a signal of its own with equally dissonant consequences. Yet in the end, roughly but surely, the dissonances die out and a consensus of sorts emerges, for as George Eliot remarks at one point, not everyone is an originator, and there is a limit to the varieties of error people can fall into.

The characters move in a landscape of opinion, but those who concern us have an inner life; they can look within as well as without, and measure their sense of themselves against the world's demands and expectations. The economy of means and materials I have referred to consists in the use of the landscape of opinion as the scene of action. It does not exclude, it rather informs and gives depth to the conventional motifs and the conventional attributes of character mentioned above. A long quotation extracted from the description of Casaubon illustrates the method:

If to Dorothea Mr. Casaubon had been the mere occasion which had set alight the fine inflammable material of her youthful illusions, does it follow that he was fairly represented in the minds of those less impassioned personages who have hitherto delivered their judgements concerning him? I protest against any absolute conclusion, any prejudice derived from Mrs. Cadwallader's contempt for a neighbouring clergyman's alleged greatness of soul, or Sir James Chettam's poor opinion of his rival's legs, from Mr. Brooke's failure to elicit a companion's ideas, or from Celia's criticism of a middle-aged scholar's personal appearance. I am not sure that the greatest man of his age, if ever that solitary superlative existed, could escape these unfavourable reflections of himself in various small mirrors; and even Milton, looking for his portrait in a spoon, must submit to have the facial angle of a bumpkin. Moreover, if Mr. Casaubon, speaking for himself, has a rather chilling rhetoric, it is not therefore certain that there is no good work or fine feeling in him. Did not an immortal physicist and interpreter of hieroglyphics write detestable verse? Has the theory of the solar system been advanced by graceful manners and conversational tact? Suppose we turn from outside estimates of a man, to wonder, with keener interest, what is the report of his own consciousness about his doings or capacity; with what hindrances he is carrying on his daily labours; what fading of hopes, or what deeper fixity of self-delusion the years are marking off within him; and with what spirit he wrestles against universal pressure, which will one day be too heavy for him, and bring his heart to its final pause. Doubtless his lot is important in his own eyes: and the chief reason that we think he asks too large a place in our consideration must be our want of room for him, since we refer him to the Divine regard with perfect confidence; nay it is even held sublime for our neighbour to expect the utmost there, however little he may have got from us. Mr. Casaubon, too, was the centre of his own world; if he was liable to think others were providentially made for him, and especially to consider them in the light of their fitness for the author of a "Key to all Mythologies," this trait is not quite alien to us, and, like the other mendicant hopes of mortals, claims some of our pity.

Certain aspects of this passage invite attention. George Eliot is here gathering up a series of notations about Casaubon which have been established in dialogue. In doing so she becomes a sharply marked present voice. We have come a long way from Fielding's interposed addresses to the reader in *Tom Jones,* a long way from Dickens and Thackeray as well—Thackeray cannot step on his stage without shaking it or dwarfing it; the effect is always of diminution, a voice which condescends to or coos about the pettiness or charm of the creatures displayed, while Dickens's effects in this kind involve facing about, leaving the characters to fend for themselves while he carries on his special pleading. George Eliot, however, speaks to the issues of her own work, and addresses the reader in terms which set her above it but never to one side. In her "I protest against any absolute conclusion . . ." we find a gentle schoolmistress's irony which places her between the book and our apprehension of it. In this instance she is saying that we are guilty, not because we are all egocentrics by definition, but because these notations about Casaubon have indeed composed our picture of him. She goes on to indicate what she is about to do with the figure: we shall end by finding him pathetic; we are to be converted—to be forced to abandon the stereotyped social gesture which leads us to "refer him [Casaubon] to the Divine regard" and refer him instead to our own failures to get the world to concede our majesty. Her own rhetoric, the somewhat heavy verbal play of "solitary superlative," the clinical remoteness and buried scientific analogy of "what deeper fixity of self-delusion the years are marking off within him," the carefully indicated central image of the mutually mirroring selves, the fact that she is playing prologue to her own action—for each of her generalities is a forecast of a part of Casaubon's fate—are all elements of that voice which frames the whole book.

Within this frame the dialogue presents dramatically the same interplay between opinion and self-regard, mirror and mirrored self. In the chapter from which the long quotation above is drawn, Lydgate encounters Dorothea for the first time. What he sees and fails to see is indicative of his angle of vision and of part of the truth about the elder Miss Brooke:

> "She is a good creature—that—fine girl—but a little too earnest," he thought. "It is troublesome to talk to such women. They are always wanting reasons, yet they are too ignorant to understand the merits of any question, and usually fall back on their moral sense to settle things after their own taste."

Each leading character has a serious delusion: Dorothea's belief that she can do good through learning; Lydgate's that the demands of science are compatible with those that Middlemarch makes of its physicians; Mr. Casaubon's idea that marriage with a beautiful and passionate young girl will bring him pleasure and repose; Bulstrode's belief that he can make an inward moral restitution for the act of misappropriating his original fortune. As Farebrother (who, along with Mary Garth, sometimes functions as a surrogate for the novelist's voice) says to Lydgate (who has been preaching his medical ideals):

> Your scheme is a good deal more difficult to carry out than the Pythagorean community though. You have not only got the old Adam in yourself against you, but you have got all those descendants of the original Adam who form the society around you.

Some of George Eliot's devices to enforce her view of the landscape of opinion are transparently such. Young Fred Vincy has long held expectations based on old Peter Featherstone's will. Peter, who lives to torment his relatives, teases him about a story that he has been trying to borrow money on post-obits. Fred is instructed to get a letter from the stiff-necked Bulstrode to the effect that this is not true.

> "You must be joking, sir. Mr. Bulstrode, like other men, believes scores of things that are not true, and he has a prejudice against me. I could easily get him to write that he knew no facts in proof of the report you speak of, though it might lead to unpleasantness. But I could hardly ask him to write down what he believes or does not believe about me."

Old Featherstone is here made to demand of Fred Vincy more than Bulstrode's testimony as to the *facts;* had he limited himself to this Fred would be less uncomfortable—but what has actually been demanded is an account of the way in which Fred is envisioned by another man—an account of one facet of his social being. The imaginative coherence of *Middlemarch* is observable on many levels; in this instance old Featherstone's demand is the counterpart of what chiefly obsesses his last months: the effect that another document, his will, will have on those who survive him. *His* opinion will emerge when his last will is read, and it will comfort no one on the *Middlemarch* scene. Fred, meanwhile, is buoyed up by an opinion generally held that he will inherit from old Featherstone: "In fact, tacit expectations of what would be done for him by Uncle Featherstone determined the angle at which most people viewed Fred Vincy in Middlemarch; and in his own consciousness, what Uncle Featherstone would do for him in an emergency, or what he would do simply as an incorporated luck, formed always an immeasurable depth of aerial perspective."

Fred is the son of a ruddy, genial merchant who is shortly to become mayor of the town, and it is part of the pattern that the elder Vincy's sense of self is more completely dependent on the views that others hold of him than that of any other character. When Bulstrode, his brother-in-law, scolds him for training Fred for the Church on simply worldly grounds, his inward reaction is described in this way: "When a man has the immediate prospect of being mayor, and is ready, in the interests of commerce, to take up a firm attitude on politics generally, he has naturally a sense of his importance to the framework of things which seems to throw questions of private conduct into the background." When Wrench, the family doctor, fails to diagnose Fred's typhoid fever Mr. Vincy feels indignant: "What Mr. Vincy thought confusedly was, that the fever might somehow have been hindered if Wrench had shown the proper solicitude about his—the Mayor's—family."

When men and affairs do not conspire to supply his self-love, the elder Vincy very quickly loses his head. Old Featherstone's latest will brings Fred nothing, and the father's view of the son changes instantly: "He's an uncommonly unfortunate lad, is Fred. He'd need have some luck by-and-by to make up for all this—else I don't know who'd have an eldest son."

Fred's own sense of the way in which the world ought to respond to the desires of a young man in his position in life has been fostered by the father who rejects him. He has long been fond of Mary Garth; this affection and the more effectual fatherhood of Caleb Garth rescue him from the family delusion that the world will cater to their handsome children. Caleb Garth is strongly reminiscent of the novelist's father, Robert Evans. He is wholly committed to the religion of "business," by which he means the actual performance of work. In Middlemarch he stands very much alone. It is not the least important of George Eliot's observations about this community that it lacks the instinct of workmanship and the pleasure in a job well done. We hear of shoddy cloth, inferior dyestuffs, oppressed weavers, ill-housed tenants, and all these things are comments on the adequacy of the landscape of opinion; it is very badly and weakly rooted in nature.

Moreover, it can show few explicit principles. Most of those who advance moral or political convictions are shown to be riding a hobby or exhibiting a personal foible. Mrs. Cadwallader is exceedingly well-born and—of necessity—very close-fisted. As the wife of a country parson, she functions admirably. But prick her to generalization and you will get either pride of birth or stinginess exemplified. So it goes in and about Middlemarch. Old Peter Featherstone has made it out that God is on the side of those who want land and cattle, though the devil backs (for a time) such "speckilating" fellows as Bulstrode. The labourers at Frick who are incited to chase away a party of railroad surveyors, and Dagley, Mr. Brooke's tenant, who defies his bad landlord in the name of "rinform," have no more comprehension of railroads or of Brooke than Brooke has of those who stand below him in the Middlemarch scale. Politics share the same obscurity. Middlemarch knows how to manipulate the Middlemarch voter; how to discomfit the bumbling Brooke on the occasion of the nominations for Parliament, but it has no sense of the national meaning of the Reform Bill. There is shrewdness on many levels, but respect for accuracy, dispassionate judgement, are confined to the Garths and Farebrother, persons who are of little consequence on the Middlemarch scene. The other character whose judgement and information are offered as authoritative is Casaubon's cousin, Will Ladislaw, who marries Dorothea after her husband's death. He, however, is so alien to Middlemarch that he cannot act on it directly: the principles, ideas, and standards which prevail in the wider world outside Middlemarch cannot be articulated within it. The medium is too dense; it is not permeable from without.

Joan Bennett, in her sensible little book on the novelist, emphasizes George Eliot's observation about the medium in which her characters move: "It is the habit of my imagination to strive after as full a vision of the medium in which character moves as of the character itself" (Cross, II, 10). *Middlemarch* authorizes an extension of this principle; George Eliot has created a common medium which completely immerses most of the characters. It is hard to conceive how an individual can on this scene really originate anything. Dorothea's wide charity finds no direct expression; Lydgate's scientific interest in the town's health meets blank incomprehension and effectual resistance, not only from all ranks in the medical hierarchy but from almost every element in the town. Indeed, the reader may by now feel (partly because I have played down the humour of the book) that Middlemarch is as oppressive as that provincial town inhabited by Emma Bovary in another study of the *mœurs de province*. In Flaubert's book there are at least the passionate impulses of Emma to combat her stifling world. What is there here?

Professor Haight, in his introduction to a recent edition of *Middlemarch*, repudiates the figure of the Wise Woman, which he finds rampant in John Walter Cross's biography. It seems to him too heavy, too statuesque, to refer to George Eliot. However, George Eliot herself is partly responsible for the dissemination of this image (she aided the compiler of a book of wise and tender sayings from her work), and the Wise Woman, or whatever we wish to call her, is an indispensable figure in discussing her work. In fact, the only thing which can possibly balance, can possibly support *Middlemarch*, is this image of the writer which the novel creates in the reader. Were she not there we should not be attending.

George Eliot is present as the only fully realized individual in her book. This sounds like a harsh saying, but it may not be quite so harsh as it sounds. When one is reading *Middlemarch* there are many moments when one looks up and says, "How intelligent, how penetrating this woman is!" And, of course, one is speaking of George Eliot. In reading the fine chapter of analysis which has to do with Lydgate's character and the situation in which he finds himself in Middlemarch, we come upon this passage:

He was at a starting-point which makes many a man's career a fine subject for betting, if there were any gentlemen given to that amusement who could appreciate the complicated probabilities of an arduous purpose, with all the possible thwartings and furtherings of circumstance, all the niceties of inward balance, by which a man swims and makes his point or else is carried headlong. The risk would

remain, even with close knowledge of Lydgate's character; for character too is a process and an unfolding.

Those who like *Middlemarch* take pleasure in the writer's judiciousness. They are far more tempted to invest themselves with her sensibility than they are to identify themselves with that of any of her
characters. It is notable that analytic passages like the one just
quoted predominate among those chosen for quotation from Leslie
Stephen's day to our own. The description of Caleb Garth, of
Rosamond Vincy's terrible self-absorption, of Dorothea's aspirations
and her blindness to her sister Celia's world, of Bulstrode's casuisti-
cal inner life, of Casaubon's tortured consciousness of inadequacy
—all these are analytic though all are matched by passages of
dialogue in which their substance is exemplified. Certain dramatic
scenes—that between Dorothea and Rosamond in particular—are
also favourites, but again the most familiar passage about Rosamond
seems to be that which describes her reaction to the awful, the in-
conceivable fact that there is another self in the world, one which
Ladislaw cherishes far more than hers. These fine and satisfying
analytic passages are not additions or decorations, nor do they
represent a division within George Eliot, rather they exhibit her
sense of process at work within the frame of actuality; it is her life
in the novel which lies at its heart; this is what we rejoice in. Ad-
mittedly this means that no character is freed to exist as Don
Quixote or Julien Sorel are enfranchised; the very firmness and
clarity of George Eliot's vision, extending to the edges of her canvas,
quite preclude her granting to any one of her creatures the authority
of existence. Like a goddess, she suffers them to exist in so far as
they may be known through sympathy and comprehension. No more
life than this can emerge—any further measure would make her
characters novelists. Those who are her surrogates, her delegated
voices, are in a sense independent of her, but they are wholly caught
up within a system of morally and aesthetically statable responses—
as is Mary Garth—and correspond rather to Mary Anne Evans, who
had once lived within a provincial society, than to George Eliot,
the novelist.

Those who live completely within the shelter of a community
never apprehend it as an entity. In a sense, the very notion of 'so-

ciety' came to imaginative fulfilment for the first time in nineteenth-century romanticism; the assumption of one of the roles of the romantic involved a reciprocal identification: here am I, a discriminable self, there is the world, the other to which I stand opposed. Of course such opposition was never total; the romantic was forced to call on some aspect of existence for support and sanction—on nature, on the philosophic status of the imagination, on libertarian politics, on the wider experience of the remote and exotic—whatever might give poetic actuality to the insights of the self. To George Eliot, a member of a succeeding generation, all these options were familiar, but none of them was acceptable. The experience which gave society objectivity for her was the loss of her religious faith. And the striking thing is that she did not thereupon become a rationalist, a scientific blue-stocking, or a lecturer on the rights of women. Only a few months after she had informed her father that she could not in conscience accompany him to church she realized that her fresh point of view towards the meaning of religion made such gestures unnecessary and foolish. She had made a massive discovery.

This discovery was very simple, but its effects were profound. Miss Evans repossessed the world imaginatively when she came to the conclusion that the creeds, formulae, practices, and institutions in which people shrouded themselves were no less significant if one saw that they were not absolute. With a feminine directness she now accepted everything she had momentarily rejected. But human behaviour was now seen as a set of symbolic gestures expressive of individual needs and desires. The positivism of Auguste Comte undoubtedly played a role in this, but it did not teach her to interpret human actions; it is clear that this was a spontaneous gift which was hers before she began to write fiction. She was able to see the emotional concomitants of churchgoing; able to make out what Diderot calls the "professional idioms" of behaviour. Each of us is like the marine animal which borrows a shell; we borrow our shells for social purposes, but our feelers wave no less expressively for that. George Eliot found that she could translate the psychic gestures involved in our religion, our politics, our superstitions, our local traditions, and discover, as she had in herself, a common root of action and reaction. She wrote to the American novelist, Harriet Beecher

Stowe, that her novel, *Oldtown Folks,* showed a comprehension of the "mixed moral influence shed on society by dogmatic systems," which was "rare even among writers." She saw, in other words, that the interplay between creeds, ideas, and desires was the novelist's business. But we must still ask what binds the novelist's world together? What sanction remains after the absoluteness of creeds and institutions has been denied?

A curious inversion in a sentence from the "Prelude" to *Middlemarch* which has been quoted above supplies an answer. In speaking of those whose career resembles Dorothea's, George Eliot remarks that the "later-born Theresas were helped by no coherent social faith and order which could perform the function of knowledge for the ardently willing soul." There is a suggestion here that if you find fulfilment through knowledge you do not need the pressure of an unquestioned social order and religious faith to sustain you. This brave assumption was written into George Eliot's work and acted out in her life. Her role as novelist involved finding and telling the truth. It was not a matter of occasional didactic interjections, but of a continuously present intelligence speaking in the declarative.

There is a famous sentence descriptive of Lydgate's character which will serve as a leading instance:

> Lydgate's spots of commonness lay in the complexion of his prejudices, which in spite of noble intention and sympathy, were half of them such as are found in ordinary men of the world: that distinction of mind which belonged to his intellectual ardour, did not penetrate his feeling and judgement about furniture, or women, or the desirability of its being known (without his telling) that he was better born than other country surgeons.

The scenes in which Lydgate's character is rendered in dialogue do not have the power of this passage of commentary. The dialogue cannot render as much as George Eliot can see. I do not mean that we are not persuaded by her statement or that we feel that dialogue and statement are not in accord; it is simply the fact that she scores most heavily as commentator that we must recognize. The very best things in George Eliot are no doubt her account of Lydgate, Rosamond, and their marriage, in *Middlemarch,* the encounters between Mrs. Transome and her former lover, Matthew Jermyn, in *Felix Holt,* and the story of Gwendolen Harleth's struggle with

Grandcourt in *Daniel Deronda*. In each case it is the voice of George Eliot the writer which is finally persuasive. It is absurd to say, as a good many people have, that her insight is intrusive or an aesthetic impropriety; it is her genius made manifest.

Middlemarch, the scene of this novel, is wholly dominated by the finely tempered mind which envisions it. But how is this scene framed and judged from without? What are the effectual boundaries of the landscape of opinion? The town—though it is a middling place from the point of view of one considering a group of provincial towns—lies on the marches, it is on the periphery of the great world, not simply the world of London or even Rome, but the world of science, the arts, and of history; realized human greatness does not enter it. We must inquire how the writer who herself moved in the great world acknowledged that world in *Middlemarch*.

There is a finely scaled scene in *Daniel Deronda* in which Gwendolen Harleth asks the musician, Klesmer, to help her to launch a musical career on nothing more than a feeble talent and her social pretensions. Klesmer confronts Gwendolen with the audacity and the ignorance of her claim. The scene has a wonderfully tonic effect —it is as if George Eliot had managed a dramatic confrontation of the austerities of art with the blind abundant energies of youth and beauty. Klesmer's treatment of Gwendolen is exquisitely modulated; it is at once a denunciation and a tribute to her as a woman. But she must be told that social lies and politeness have nothing to do with being an artist. In the world of art you must tell the truth; self-regard and the world's opinion must give way before realized mastery. There is an analogous scene in *Middlemarch,* though the standard invoked is not impersonal. Rosemary's flirtation with Ladislaw is abruptly ended when she discovers that Dorothea is all-important to him. She had found in Ladislaw a representative of the world outside Middlemarch to which she had ignorantly aspired, and Ladislaw thinks her of no account. She is momentarily awed into a generosity which brings Ladislaw and Dorothea together. Throughout the book Ladislaw speaks authoritatively about the world outside the town's awareness. It is he who tells Dorothea that Casaubon's work is useless because he has not read the German scholars; it is he who demands fidelity to a standard of artistic accomplishment; he alone has some sense of national politics.

Yet Ladislaw does not have the authority of Klesmer; he is the weakest of the major characters, not merely because he is made to behave like a dilettante, but because George Eliot's judiciousness does not extend to him; he is not understood. In fact, he is rather like a character in an ordinary novel. F. R. Leavis sees this as a consequence of the weakness of the figure of Dorothea. Since she is in part a self-indulgent fantasy of George Eliot's and not wholly disciplined by the demands of the novel, we may think of Ladislaw as an accessory required by the fantasy. Certainly the scenes they share are full of high-flown nonsense. But there is a good deal of evidence that Dorothea and Ladislaw represent something more than the unresolved longings of Mary Anne Evans. The leading characters in *Romola, Felix Holt, Middlemarch,* and *Daniel Deronda* all escape the circle of the author's judgement. It is claimed for each of them that they aspire to or escape into the great world. Dorothea is the partial exception. When confronted by her uncle, Casaubon, her sister Celia, or the Chettams, she is fully controlled, fully understood. But Romola, Felix Holt, and Deronda are all extravagantly moral or extravagantly spiritual or both. And Dorothea and Ladislaw in their scenes together have the same defect.

Instead of thinking of *Middlemarch* as showing two strains, an artistically responsible element and a neurotically compelled one, we must, I believe, adopt a fresh version of the traditional assertion that George Eliot's conception of her fiction is internally divided. Leavis has pointed to the meaninglessness of the form this assertion of a split took in the criticism of Henry James and Leslie Stephen. The disjunction between an "intellectual" George Eliot and a George Eliot who has the novelist's sympathetic comprehension of human beings is, as we have seen, a clear-cut contradiction. It is the voice heard within the frame of her best fiction which has high intellectual distinction.

But there is an internal division in her conception of *Middlemarch* which corresponds to the far more serious split in *Daniel Deronda,* in which Deronda's mystical religiosity is given precedence over the fictionally superior story of Gwendolen Harleth. (The argument may also be applied to *Romola* and *Felix Holt.*) This split in the writer's conception of fiction appears to have a biographical root. The novels of George Eliot's maturity re-enact her own emancipation;

the values which the Garths and Farebrother assert within the little world of Middlemarch are reasserted from the viewpoint of liberated intelligence by the voice of the narrator; her loss of faith, her translation to the metropolis, her defiance of propriety in living with Lewes, are all justified by the activity of the novelist who surveys Middlemarch. The right opinion of the Garths and Farebrother gives way before the knowledge of the novelist. But for George Eliot the re-enactment brought with it an irresistible impulse to include a character who could function as knower, an *embodied* voice.

She was unable, even in the years of her maturest art, to conceive of fiction as a truly independent form. It would seem to have been enough to bring that fine intelligence to bear on the enclosed world of Middlemarch, but she is never content with this. She must bring forward some instance of principled nonconformity, as if to feed an appetite for self-justification. We must conclude, I think, that the fairy-tale triumph of Romola over the physical and moral ills of a fever-stricken village, and the fantastic errand which takes Deronda to Jerusalem—he is, in effect, to build a culture!—are not merely tributes to a Victorian taste for moral exaltation. They are attempts on the part of the writer to give herself a recognizable moral status.

The English novel is so much the richer for George Eliot's contribution that one may be tempted into scolding her for not doing what no English novelist of the century did: for not taking possession of the great world. Her sense of community, her finely modulated articulation of passion and idea, the clarity and firmness of her characterization—these things alone justify Virginia Woolf's remark that *Middlemarch* was one of the few English novels written for grown-up people. Since the grown-up perspective includes Flaubert and Tolstoy, we are of course conscious that George Eliot did not share their power to incarnate the great world in the lesser one, to make the novel an instrument which can register the fate of a society in the perspective of history and heroic achievement. To exercise this power she would have had to take her own splendid powers for granted, and this she could not do.

Daniel Deronda: A Conversation

by Henry James

Theodora, one day early in the autumn, sat on her piazza with a piece of embroidery, the design of which she invented as she proceeded, being careful, however, to have a Japanese screen before her, to keep her inspiration at the proper altitude. Pulcheria, who was paying her a visit, sat near her with a closed book, in a paper cover, in her lap. Pulcheria was playing with the little dog, rather idly, but Theodora was stitching, steadily and meditatively. "Well," said Theodora, at last, "I wonder what he accomplished in the East." Pulcheria took the little dog into her lap and made him sit on the book. "Oh," she replied, "they had tea-parties at Jerusalem, —exclusively of ladies,—and he sat in the midst and stirred his tea and made high-toned remarks. And then Mirah sang a little, just a little, on account of her voice being so weak. Sit still, Fido," she continued, addressing the little dog, "and keep your nose out of my face. But it's a nice little nose, all the same," she pursued, "a nice little short snub nose, and not a horrid big Jewish nose. Oh, my dear, when I think what a collection of noses there must have been at that wedding!" At this moment Constantius steps out upon the piazza from the long parlor window, hat and stick in hand and his shoes a trifle dusty. He has some steps to take before he reaches the end of the piazza where the ladies are sitting, and this gives Pulcheria time to murmur, "Talk of snub noses!" Constantius is presented by Theodora to Pulcheria, and he sits down and exclaims upon the admirable blueness of the sea, which lies in a straight band across the green of the little lawn; comments too upon the pleasure of having one side of one's piazza in the shade. Soon Fido, the little

"*Daniel Deronda:* A Conversation" by Henry James. From *The Atlantic Monthly*, 38 (December, 1876), 684–94.

dog, still restless, jumps off Pulcheria's lap and reveals the book, which lies title upward. "Oh," says Constantius, "you have been finishing Daniel Deronda?" Then follows a conversation which it will be more convenient to present in another form.

Theodora. Yes, Pulcheria has been reading aloud the last chapters to me. They are wonderfully beautiful.

Constantius (after a moment's hesitation). Yes, they are very beautiful. I am sure you read well, Pulcheria, to give the fine passages their full value.

Theodora. She reads well when she chooses, but I am sorry to say that in some of the fine passages of this last book she took quite a false tone. I couldn't have read them aloud, myself; I should have broken down. But Pulcheria,—would you really believe it?— when she couldn't go on, it was not for tears, but for—the contrary.

Constantius. For smiles? Did you really find it comical? One of my objections to Daniel Deronda is the absence of those delightfully humorous passages which enlivened the author's former works.

Pulcheria. Oh, I think there are some places as amusing as anything in Adam Bede or The Mill on the Floss: for instance, where, at the last, Deronda wipes Gwendolen's tears and Gwendolen wipes his.

Constantius. Yes, I know what you mean. I can understand that situation presenting a slightly ridiculous image; that is, if the current of the story does not swiftly carry you past that idea.

Pulcheria. What do you mean by the current of the story? I never read a story with less current. It is not a river; it is a series of lakes. I once read of a group of little uneven ponds resembling, from a bird's-eye view, a looking-glass which had fallen upon the floor and broken, and was lying in fragments. That is what Daniel Deronda would look like, on a bird's-eye view.

Theodora. Pulcheria found that comparison in a French novel. She is always reading French novels.

Constantius. Ah, there are some very good ones.

Pulcheria (perversely). I don't know; I think there are some very poor ones.

Constantius. The comparison is not bad, at any rate. I know what you mean by Daniel Deronda lacking current. It has almost as little as Romola.

Pulcheria. Oh, Romola is unpardonably slow; it absolutely stagnates.

Constantius. Yes, I know what you mean by that. But I am afraid you are not friendly to our great novelist.

Theodora. She likes Balzac and George Sand and other impure writers.

Constantius. Well, I must say I understand that.

Pulcheria. My favorite novelist is Thackeray, and I am extremely fond of Miss Austen.

Constantius. I understand that, too. You read over The Newcomes and Pride and Prejudice.

Pulcheria. No, I don't read them over, now; I think them over. I have been making visits for a long time past to a series of friends, and I have spent the last six months in reading Daniel Deronda aloud. Fortune would have it that I should always arrive by the same train as the new number. I am considered a frivolous, idle creature; I am not a disciple in the new school of embroidery, like Theodora; so I was immediately pushed into a chair and the book thrust into my hand, that I might lift up my voice and make peace between all the impatiences that were snatching at it. So I may claim at least that I have read every word of the work. I never skipped.

Theodora. I should hope not, indeed!

Constantius. And do you mean that you really didn't enjoy it?

Pulcheria. I found it protracted, pretentious, pedantic.

Constantius. I see; I can understand that.

Theodora. Oh, you understand too much! Here is the twentieth time you have used that formula.

Constantius. What will you have? You know I must try to understand, it's my trade.

Theodora. He means he writes reviews. Trying *not* to understand is what I call that trade!

Constantius. Say, then, I take it the wrong way; that is why it has never made my fortune. But I do try to understand; it is my—my— (He pauses.)

Theodora. I know what you want to say. Your strong side.

Pulcheria. And what is his weak side?

Theodora. He writes novels.

Constantius. I have written *one*. You can't call that a side.

Pulcheria. I should like to read it,—not aloud!

Constantius. You can't read it softly enough. But you, Theodora, you didn't find our book too "protracted"?

Theodora. I should have liked it to continue indefinitely, to keep coming out always, to be one of the regular things of life.

Pulcheria. Oh, come here, little dog! To think that Daniel Deronda might be perpetual when you, little short-nosed darling, can't last at the most more than eight or nine years!

Theodora. A book like Daniel Deronda becomes part of one's life; one lives in it or alongside of it. I don't hesitate to say that I have been living in this one for the last eight months. It is such a complete world George Eliot builds up; it is so vast, so much-embracing! It has such a firm earth and such an ethereal sky. You can turn into it and lose yourself in it.

Pulcheria. Oh, easily, and die of cold and starvation!

Theodora. I have been very near to poor Gwendolen and very near to dear little Mirah. And the dear little Meyricks, also; I know them intimately well.

Pulcheria. The Meyricks, I grant you, are the best thing in the book.

Theodora. They are a delicious family; I wish they lived in Boston. I consider Herr Klesmer almost Shakespearian, and his wife is almost as good. I have been near to poor, grand Mordecai—

Pulcheria. Oh, reflect, my dear; not too near.

Theodora. And as for Deronda himself, I freely confess that I am consumed with a hopeless passion for him. He is the most irresistible man in the literature of fiction.

Pulcheria. He is not a man at all!

Theodora. I remember nothing more beautiful than the description of his childhood, and that picture of his lying on the grass in the abbey cloister, a beautiful seraph-faced boy, with a lovely voice, reading history and asking his Scotch tutor why the Popes had so many nephews. He must have been delightfully handsome.

Pulcheria. Never, my dear, with that nose! I am sure he had a nose, and I hold that the author has shown great pusillanimity in her treatment of it. She has quite shirked it. The picture you speak of is very pretty, but a picture is not a person. And why is he always grasping his coat-collar, as if he wished to hang himself up? The author had an uncomfortable feeling that she must make him do something real, something visible and sensible, and she hit upon that awkward device. I don't see what you mean by saying you have been *near* those people; that is just what one is not. They produce no illusion. They are described and analyzed to death, but we don't see them or hear them or touch them. Deronda clutches his coat-collar. Mirah crosses her feet, and Mordecai talks like the Bible; but that doesn't make real figures of them. They have no existence outside of the author's study.

Theodora. If you mean that they are nobly imaginative, I quite agree with you; and if they say nothing to your own imagination, the fault is yours, not theirs.

Pulcheria. Pray don't say they are Shakespearian again. Shakespeare went to work another way.

Constantius. I think you are both in a measure right; there is a distinction to be drawn. There are in Daniel Deronda the figures based upon observation and the figures based upon invention. This distinction, I know, is rather a rough one. There are no figures in any novel that are pure observation and none that are pure invention. But either element may preponderate, and in those cases in which invention has preponderated George Eliot seems to me to have achieved at the best but so many brilliant failures.

Theodora. And are *you* turning severe? I thought you admired her so much.

Constantius. I defy any one to admire her more, but one must discriminate. Speaking brutally, I consider Daniel Deronda the weakest of her books. It strikes me as very sensibly inferior to Middlemarch. I have an immense opinion of Middlemarch.

Pulcheria. Not having been obliged by circumstances to read Middlemarch to other people, I didn't read it at all. I couldn't read it to myself. I tried, but broke down. I appreciated Rosamond, but I couldn't believe in Dorothea.

Theodora (very gravely). So much the worse for you, Pulcheria. I have enjoyed Daniel Deronda *because* I had enjoyed Middlemarch. Why should you throw Middlemarch up against her? It seems to me that if a book is fine it is fine. I have enjoyed Deronda deeply, from beginning to end.

Constantius. I assure you, so have I. I can read nothing of George Eliot's without enjoyment. I even enjoy her poetry, though I don't approve of it. In whatever she writes I enjoy her mind—her large, luminous, airy mind. The intellectual brilliancy of Daniel Deronda strikes me as very great, in excess of anything the author had done. In the first couple of numbers of the book this ravished me. I delighted in its tone, its deep, rich English tone, in which so many notes seemed melted together.

Pulcheria. The tone is not English, it is German.

Constantius. I understand that—if Theodora will allow me to say so. Little by little I began to feel that I cared less for certain notes than for others. I say it under my breath—I began to feel an occasional temptation to skip. Roughly speaking, all the Jewish burden of the story tended to weary me; it is this part that produces the small illusion which I agree with Pulcheria in finding. Gwendolen and Grandcourt are admirable. Gwendolen is a masterpiece. She is known, felt, and presented, psychologically, altogether in the grand manner. Beside her and beside her husband—a consummate picture of English brutality refined and distilled (for Grandcourt is before all things brutal)—Deronda, Mordecai, and Mirah are hardly more than shadows. They and their fortunes are all improvisation. I don't say anything against improvisation. When it succeeds it has a surpassing charm. But it must succeed. With George Eliot it seems to me to succeed only partially, less than one would expect of her talent. The story of Deronda's life, his mother's story, Mirah's story, are quite the sort of thing one finds in George Sand. But they are really not so good as they would be in George Sand. George Sand would have carried it off with a lighter hand.

Theodora. Oh, Constantius, how can you compare George Eliot's novels to that woman's? It is sunlight and moonshine.

Pulcheria. I really think the two writers are very much alike. They are both very voluble, both addicted to moralizing and philosophizing *à tout bout de champ,* both inartistic!

Constantius. I see what you mean. But George Eliot is solid and George Sand is liquid. When occasionally George Eliot liquefies,—as in the history of Deronda's birth, and in that of Mirah,—it is not to as crystalline a clearness as the author of Consuelo and André. Take Mirah's long narrative of her adventures, when she unfolds them to Mrs. Meyrick. It is arranged, it is artificial, old-fashioned, quite in the George Sand manner. But George Sand would have done it better. The false tone would have remained, but it would have been more persuasive. It would have been a fib, but the fib would have been neater.

Theodora. I don't think fibbing neatly a merit; and I don't see what is to be gained by such comparisons. George Eliot is pure and George Sand is impure; how can you compare them? As for the Jewish element in Deronda, I think it a very fine idea; it's a noble subject. Wilkie Collins and Miss Braddon would not have thought of it, but that does not condemn it. It shows a large conception of what one may do in a novel. I heard you say, the other day, that most novels were so trivial—that they had no general ideas. Here is a general idea, the idea interpreted by Deronda. I have never disliked the Jews, as some people do; I am not like Pulcheria, who sees a Jew in every bush. I wish there were one; I would cultivate shrubbery! I have known too many clever and charming Jews; I have known none that were not clever.

Pulcheria. Clever, but not charming!

Constantius. I quite agree with you as to Deronda's going in for the Jews and turning out a Jew himself being a fine subject, and this quite apart from the fact of whether such a thing as a Jewish revival is at all a possibility. If it is a possibility, so much the better—so much the better for the subject, I mean.

Pulcheria. A la bonne heure!

Constantius. I rather suspect it is not a possibility; that the Jews in general take themselves much less seriously than that. They have other fish to fry! George Eliot takes them as a person outside of Judaism—picturesquely. I don't believe that is the way they take themselves.

Pulcheria. They have the less excuse, then, for keeping themselves so dirty.

Theodora. George Eliot must have known some delightful Jews!

Constantius. Very likely; but I shouldn't wonder if the most delightful of them had smiled a trifle, here and there, over her book. But that makes nothing, as Herr Klesmer would say. The subject is a noble one. The idea of depicting a nature able to feel and worthy to feel the sort of inspiration that takes possession of Deronda, of depicting it sympathetically, minutely, and intimately—such an idea has great elevation. There is something very fascinating in the mission that Deronda takes upon himself. I don't quite know what it means, I don't understand more than half of Mordecai's rhapsodies, and I don't perceive exactly what practical steps could be taken. Deronda could go about and talk with clever Jews—not an unpleasant life.

Pulcheria. All that seems to me so unreal that when at the end the author finds herself confronted with the necessity of making him start for the East by the train, and announces that Sir Hugo and Lady Mallinger have given his wife "a complete Eastern outfit," I descend to the ground with a ludicrous jump.

Constantius. Unreal if you please; that is no objection to it; it greatly tickles my imagination. I like extremely the idea of Mordecai believing, without ground of belief, that if he only waits, a young man on whom nature and society have centred all their gifts will come to him and receive from his hands the precious vessel of his hopes. It is romantic, but it is not vulgar romance; it is finely romantic. And there is something very fine in the author's own feeling about Deronda. He is a very generous creation. He is, I think, a failure—a brilliant failure; if he had been a success I would call him a splendid creation. The author meant to do things very handsomely for him; she meant, apparently, to make a faultless human being.

Pulcheria. She made a dreadful prig.

Constantius. He *is* rather priggish, and one wonders that so clever a woman as George Eliot shouldn't see it.

Pulcheria. He has no blood in his body. His attitude at moments absolutely trenches on the farcical.

Theodora. Pulcheria likes the little gentlemen in the French novels who take good care of their attitudes, which are always the same attitude, the attitude of "conquest," and of a conquest that tickles their vanity. Deronda has a contour that cuts straight through the middle of all that. He is made of a stuff that isn't dreamt of in their philosophy.

Pulcheria. Pulcheria likes very much a novel which she read three or four years ago, but which she has not forgotten. It was by Ivan Tourguéneff, and it was called On the Eve. Theodora has read it, I know, because she admires Tourguéneff, and Constantius has read it, I suppose, because he has read everything.

Constantius. If I had no reason but that for my reading, it would be small. But Tourguéneff is my man.

Pulcheria. You were just now praising George Eliot's general ideas. The tale of which I speak contains in the portrait of the hero very much such a general idea as you find in the portrait of Deronda. Don't you remember the young Bulgarian student, Inssaroff, who gives himself the mission of rescuing his country from its subjection to the Turks? Poor man, if he had foreseen the horrible summer of 1876! His character is the picture of a race-passion, of patriotic hopes and dreams. But what a difference in the vividness of the two figures. Inssaroff is a man; he stands up on his feet; we see him, hear him, and touch him. And it has taken the author but a couple of hundred pages—not eight volumes—to do it!

Theodora. I don't remember Inssaroff at all, but I perfectly remember the heroine, Elena. She is certainly most remarkable, but, remarkable as she is, I should never dream of calling her so wonderful as Gwendolen.

Constantius. Tourguéneff is a magician, which I don't think I should call George Eliot. One is a poet, the other is a philosopher. One cares for the reason of things and the other cares for the aspect of things. George Eliot, in embarking with Deronda, took aboard, as it were, a far heavier cargo than Tourguéneff with his Inssaroff. She proposed, consciously, to strike more notes.

Pulcheria. Oh, consciously, yes!

Constantius. George Eliot wished to show the possible picturesqueness—

the romance, as it were—of a high moral tone. Deronda is a moralist, a moralist with a rich complexion.

Theodora. It is a most beautiful nature. I don't know anywhere a more complete, a more deeply analyzed portrait of a great nature. We praise novelists for wandering and creeping so into the small corners of the mind. That is what we praise Balzac for when he gets down upon all fours to crawl through the Père Goriot or the Parents Pauvres. But I must say I think it a finer thing to unlock with as firm a hand as George Eliot some of the greater chambers of human character. Deronda is in a manner an ideal character, if you will, but he seems to me triumphantly married to reality. There are some admirable things said about him; nothing can be finer than those pages of description of his moral temperament in the fourth book—his elevated way of looking at things, his impartiality, his universal sympathy, and at the same time his fear of their turning into mere irresponsible indifference. I remember some of it verbally: "He was ceasing to care for knowledge—he had no ambition for practice—unless they could be gathered up into one current with his emotions."

Pulcheria. Oh, there is plenty about his emotions. Everything about him is "emotive." That bad word occurs on every fifth page.

Theodora. I don't see that it is a bad word.

Pulcheria. It may be good German, but it is poor English.

Theodora. It is not German at all; it is Latin. So, my dear!

Pulcheria. As I say, then, it is not English.

Theodora. This is the first time I ever heard that George Eliot's style was bad!

Constantius. It is admirable; it has the most delightful and the most intellectually comfortable suggestions. But it is occasionally a little too long-sleeved, as I may say. It is sometimes too loose a fit for the thought, a little baggy.

Theodora. And the advice he gives Gwendolen, the things he says to her, they are the very essence of wisdom, of warm human wisdom, knowing life and feeling it. "Keep your fears as a safeguard, it may make consequences passionately present to you." What can be better than that?

Pulcheria. Nothing, perhaps. But what can be drearier than a novel in which the function of the hero—young, handsome, and brilliant—is to give didactic advice, in a proverbial form, to the young, beautiful, and brilliant heroine?

Constantius. That is not putting it quite fairly. The function of

Deronda is to have Gwendolen fall in love with him, to say nothing
of falling in love himself with Mirah.

Pulcheria. Yes, the less said about that the better. All we know about
Mirah is that she has delicate rings of hair, sits with her feet crossed,
and talks like a book.

Constantius. Deronda's function of adviser to Gwendolen does not
strike me as so ridiculous. He is not nearly so ridiculous as if he
were lovesick. It is a very interesting situation—that of a man with
whom a beautiful woman in trouble falls in love, and yet whose
affections are so preoccupied that the most he can do for her in
return is to enter kindly and sympathetically into her position, pity
her, and talk to her. George Eliot always gives us something that
is strikingly and ironically characteristic of human life; and what
savors more of the essential crookedness of human fortune than the
sad cross-purposes of these two young people? Poor Gwendolen's
falling in love with Deronda is part of her own luckless history,
not of his.

Theodora. I do think he takes it to himself rather too little. No man
had ever so little vanity.

Pulcheria. It is very inconsistent, therefore, as well as being extremely
impertinent and ill-mannered, his buying back and sending to her
her necklace at Leubronn.

Constantius. Oh, you must concede that; without it there would have
been no story. A man writing of him, however would certainly have
made him more peccable. As George Eliot lets herself go about him
she becomes delightfully, almost touchingly feminine. It is like her
making Romola go to housekeeping with Tessa, after Tito Melema's
death; like her making Dorothea marry Will Ladislaw. If Dorothea
had married any one after her misadventure with Casaubon, she
would have married a hussar!

Theodora. Perhaps some day Gwendolen will marry Rex.

Pulcheria. Pray, who is Rex?

Theodora. Why, Pulcheria, how can you forget?

Pulcheria. Nay, how can I remember? But I recall such a name in the
dim antiquity of the first or second book. Yes, and then he is pushed
to the front again at the last, just in time not to miss the falling
of the curtain. Gwendolen will certainly not have the audacity to
marry any one we know so little about.

Constantius. I have been wanting to say that there seems to me to be
two very distinct elements in George Eliot—a spontaneous one and
an artificial one. There is what she is by inspiration, and what she is

because it is expected of her. These two heads have been very perceptible in her recent writings; they are much less noticeable in her early ones.

Theodora. You mean that she is too scientific? So long as she remains the great literary genius that she is, how can she be too scientific? She is simply permeated with the highest culture of the age.

Pulcheria. She talks too much about the "dynamic quality" of people's eyes. When she uses such a phrase as that in the first sentence in her book she is not a great literary genius, because she shows a want of tact. There can't be a worse limitation.

Constantius (laughing). The "dynamic quality" of Gwendolen's glance has made the tour of the world.

Theodora. It shows a very low level of culture on the world's part to be agitated by a term perfectly familiar to all decently-educated people.

Pulcheria. I don't pretend to be decently educated; pray tell me what it means.

Constantius (promptly). I think Pulcheria has hit it in speaking of a want of tact. In the manner of Daniel Deronda, throughout, there is something that one may call a want of tact. The epigraphs in verse are a want of tact; they are sometimes, I think, a trifle more pretentious than really pregnant; the importunity of the moral reflections is a want of tact; the very diffuseness of the book is a want of tact. But it comes back to what I said just now about one's sense of the author writing under a sort of external pressure. I began to notice it in Felix Holt; I don't think I had before. She strikes me as a person who certainly has naturally a taste for general considerations, but who has fallen upon an age and a circle which have compelled her to give them an exaggerated attention. She does not strike me as naturally a critic, less still as naturally a skeptic; her spontaneous part is to observe life and to feel it, to feel it with admirable depth. Contemplation, sympathy, and faith,—something like that, I should say, would have been her natural scale. If she had fallen upon an age of enthusiastic assent to old articles of faith, it seems to me possible that she would have had a more perfect, a more consistent and graceful development, than she has actually had. If she had cast herself into such a current,—her genius being equal,—it might have carried her to splendid distances. But she has chosen to go into criticism, and to the critics she addresses her work; I mean the critics of the universe. Instead of feeling life itself, it is "views" upon life that she tries to feel.

Pulcheria. Pray, how can you feel a "view"?

Constantius. I don't think you can; you had better give up trying.

Pulcheria. She is the victim of a first-class education. I am so glad!

Constantius. Thanks to her admirable intellect she philosophizes very sufficiently; but meanwhile she has given a chill to her genius. She has come near spoiling an artist.

Pulcheria. She has quite spoiled one. Or rather I shouldn't say that, because there was no artist to spoil. I maintain that she is not an artist. An artist could never have put a story together so monstrously ill. She has no sense of form.

Theodora. Pray, what could be more artistic than the way that Deronda's paternity is concealed till almost the end, and the way we are made to suppose Sir Hugo is his father?

Pulcheria. And Mirah his sister. How does that fit together? I was as little made to suppose he was not a Jew as I cared when I found out he was. And his mother popping up through a trapdoor and popping down again, at the last, in that scrambling fashion! His mother is very bad.

Constantius. I think Deronda's mother is one of the unvivified characters; she belongs to the cold half of the book. All the Jewish part is at bottom cold; that is my only objection. I have enjoyed it because my fancy often warms cold things; but beside Gwendolen's history it is like the full half of the lunar disk beside the empty one. It is admirably studied, it is imagined, it is understood; but it is not realized. One feels this strongly in just those scenes between Deronda and his mother; one feels that one has been appealed to on rather an artificial ground of interest. To make Deronda's reversion to his native faith more dramatic and profound, the author has given him a mother who on very arbitrary grounds, apparently, has separated herself from this same faith, and who has been kept waiting in the wing, as it were, for many acts, to come on and make her speech and say so. This moral situation of hers we are invited retrospectively to appreciate. But we hardly care to do so.

Pulcheria. I don't *see* the princess, in spite of her flame-colored robe. Why should an actress and prima-donna care so much about religious matters?

Theodora. It was not only that; it was the Jewish race she hated, Jewish manners and looks. You, my dear, ought to understand that.

Pulcheria. I do, but I am not a Jewish actress of genius; I am not what Rachel was. If I were, I should have other things to think about.

Constantius. Think now a little about poor Gwendolen.

Pulcheria. I don't care to think about her. She was a second-rate English girl who spoke of her mother as "my mamma," and got into a flutter about a lord.

Theodora. I don't see that she is worse than if she were a first-rate American girl, who should speak of her female parent as "mother," and get into exactly the same flutter.

Pulcheria. It wouldn't be the same flutter, at all; it wouldn't be any flutter. She wouldn't be afraid of the lord.

Theodora. I am sure I don't perceive whom Gwendolen was afraid of. She was afraid of her misdeed,—her broken promise,—after she had committed it, and through that fear she was afraid of her husband. Well she might be! I can imagine nothing more vivid than the sense we get of his absolutely *clammy* selfishness.

Pulcheria. She was not afraid of Deronda when, immediately after her marriage, and without any but the most casual acquaintance with him, she begins to hover about him at the Mallingers', and to drop little confidences about her conjugal woes. That seems to me very indelicate; ask any woman.

Constantius. The very purpose of the author is to give us an idea of the sort of confidence that Deronda inspired—its irresistible potency!

Pulcheria. A lay father-confessor. Dreadful!

Constantius. And to give us an idea also of the acuteness of Gwendolen's depression, of her haunting sense of impending trouble.

Theodora. It must be remembered that Gwendolen was in love with Deronda from the first, long before she knew it. She didn't know it, poor girl, but that was it.

Pulcheria. That makes the matter worse. It is very disagreeable to have her rustling about a man who is indifferent to her, in that fashion.

Theodora. He was not indifferent to her, since he sent her back her necklace.

Pulcheria. Of all the delicate attention to a charming girl that I ever heard of, that little pecuniary transaction is the most felicitous.

Constantius. You must remember that he had been *en rapport* with her at the gaming table. She had been playing in defiance of his observation, and he, continuing to observe her, had been in a measure responsible for her loss. There was a tacit consciousness of this between them. You may contest the possibility of tacit consciousness going so far, but that is not a serious objection. You may point out two or three weak spots in detail; the fact remains that Gwendolen's whole history is superbly told. And see how the girl is known, inside out, how thoroughly she is felt and understood! It is the most *intelligent* thing in all George Eliot's writing, and that is saying much. It is so deep, so true, so complete, it holds such a wealth of psychological detail, it is more than masterly.

Theodora. I don't know where the perception of character has sailed closer to the wind.

Pulcheria. The portrait may be admirable, but it has one little fault. You don't care a straw for the original. Gwendolen is not an interesting girl, and when the author tries to invest her with a deep tragic interest she does so at the expense of consistency. She has made her at the outset too light, too flimsy; tragedy has no hold on such a girl.

Theodora. You are hard to satisfy. You said this morning that Dorothea was too heavy, and now you find Gwendolen too light. George Eliot wished to give us the perfect counterpart of Dorothea. Having made one portrait she was worthy to make the other.

Pulcheria. She has committed the fatal error of making Gwendolen vulgarly, pettily, dryly selfish. She was *personally* selfish.

Theodora. I know nothing more personal than selfishness.

Pulcheria. I am selfish, but I don't go about with my chin out like that; at least I hope I don't. She was an odious young woman, and one can't care what becomes of her. When her marriage turned out ill she would have become still more hard and positive; to make her soft and appealing is very bad logic. The second Gwendolen doesn't belong to the first.

Constantius. She is perhaps at the first a little childish for the weight of interest she has to carry, a little too much after the pattern of the unconscientious young ladies of Miss Yonge and Miss Sewell.

Theodora. Since when is it forbidden to make one's heroine young? Gwendolen is a perfect picture of youthfulness—its eagerness, its presumption, its preoccupation with itself, its vanity and silliness, its sense of its own absoluteness. But she is extremely intelligent and clever, and therefore tragedy *can* have a hold upon her. Her conscience doesn't make the tragedy; that is an old story, and, I think, a secondary form of suffering. It is the tragedy that makes her conscience, which then reacts upon it; and I can think of nothing more powerful than the way in which the growth of her conscience is traced, nothing more touching than the picture of its helpless maturity.

Constantius. That is perfectly true. Gwendolen's history is admirably typical—as most things are with George Eliot; it is the very stuff that human life is made of. What is it made of but the discovery by each of us that we are at the best but a rather ridiculous fifth wheel to the coach, after we have sat cracking our whip and believing that we are at least the coachman in person? We think we are the main hoop to the barrel, and we turn out to be but a very incidental splinter in one of the staves. The universe, forcing itself with a slow, inexorable pressure into a narrow, complacent, and yet after all extremely sensitive mind, and making it ache with the pain of the process—that is Gwendolen's story. And it becomes completely characteristic in that her supreme perception of the fact that the world is whirling past her is in the disappointment not of a base, but of an exalted passion. The very chance to embrace what the author is so fond of calling a "larger life" seems refused to her. She is punished for being narrow and she is not allowed a chance to expand. Her finding Deronda preëngaged to go to the East and stir up the race-feeling of the Jews strikes one as a wonderfully happy invention. The irony of the situation, for poor Gwendolen, is almost grotesque, and it makes one wonder whether the whole heavy structure of the Jewish question in the story was not built up by the author for the express purpose of giving its proper force to this particular stroke.

Theodora. George Eliot's intentions are extremely complex. The mass is for each detail and each detail is for the mass.

Pulcheria. She is very fond of deaths by drowning. Maggie Tulliver and her brother are drowned, Tito Melema is drowned, Mr. Grandcourt is drowned. It is extremely unlikely that Grandcourt should not have known how to swim.

Constantius. He did, of course, but he had a cramp. It served him right. I can't imagine a more consummate representation of the most detestable kind of Englishman—the Englishman who thinks it low to articulate. And in Grandcourt the type and the individual are so happily met: the type with its sense of the proprieties, and the individual with his absence of all sense. He is the apotheosis of dryness, a human expression of the simple idea of the perpendicular.

Theodora. Mr. Casaubon in Middlemarch was very dry, too; and yet what a genius it is that can give us two disagreeable husbands who are so utterly different.

Pulcheria. You must count the two disagreeable wives, too—Rosamond Vincy and Gwendolen. They are very much alike. I know the author didn't mean it; it proves how common a type the worldly, *pincée,* illiberal young Englishwoman is. They are both disagreeable; you can't get over that.

Constantius. There is something in that, perhaps. I think, at any rate, that the secondary people here are less delightful than in Middle-

march; there is nothing so good as Mary Garth and her father, or
the little old lady who steals sugar, or the parson who is in love with
Mary, or the country relatives of old Mr. Featherstone. Rex
Gascoigne is not so good as Fred Vincy.

Theodora. Mr. Gascoigne is admirable, and Mrs. Davilow is charming.

Pulcheria. And you must not forget that you think Herr Klesmer
"Shakespearian." Wouldn't "Wagnerian" be high enough praise?

Constantius. Yes, one must make an exception with regard to the
Klesmers and the Meyricks. They are delightful, and as for Klesmer
himself, and Hans Meyrick, Theodora may maintain her epithet.
Shakespearian characters are characters that are born out of the
overflow of observation, characters that make the drama seem multi-
tudinous, like life. Klesmer comes in with a sort of Shakespearian
"value," as a painter would say, and so, in a different tone, does
Hans Meyrick. They spring from a much-peopled mind.

Theodora. I think Gwendolen's confrontation with Klesmer one of the
finest things in the book.

Constantius. It is like everything in George Eliot, it will bear thinking
of.

Pulcheria. All that is very fine, but you cannot persuade me that
Deronda is not a very awkward and ill-made story. It has nothing
that one can call a subject. A silly young girl and a heavy overwise
young man who *don't* fall in love with her! That is the *donnée* of
eight monthly volumes. I call it very flat. Is that what the exquisite
art of Thackeray and Miss Austen and Hawthorne has come to? I
would as soon read a German novel outright.

Theodora. There is something higher than form—there is spirit.

Constantius. I am afraid Pulcheria is sadly æsthetic. She had better
confine herself to Mérimée.

Pulcheria. I shall certainly to-day read over the Double Méprise.

Theodora. Oh, my dear, don't!

Constantius. Yes, I think there is little art in Deronda, but I think there
is a vast amount of life. In life without art you can find your account; but art without life is a poor affair. The book is full of the
world.

Theodora. It is full of beauty and sagacity, and there is quite art
enough for me.

Pulcheria (to the little dog). We are silenced, darling, but we are not
convinced, are we? (The dog begins to bark.) No, we are not even
silenced. It's a young woman with two bandboxes.

Theodora. Oh, it must be our muslins.

Constantius (rising to go). I see what you mean!

Chronology of Important Dates

1819   Born Mary Anne Evans, November 22, Arbury, Warwickshire, England.

1824–35   Schooling (at Griff, Attleborough, Nuneaton, and Coventry).

1836   Mother dies, February 3.

1837–47   Father's housekeeper.

1841   Becomes acquainted with the Charles Bray family of Rosehill, near Coventry.

1842   Refuses for several months to go to church with her father.

1844   Begins to translate Strauss's *Das Leben Jesu.*

1846   Translation of Strauss published as *The Life of Jesus, Critically Examined.*

1849   Begins to translate Spinoza's *Tractatus Theologico-Politicus;* father dies, May 31; accompanies the Brays to the Continent.

1850   Returns to England (March); meets John Chapman.

1851–53   For much of the time (and under difficult emotional circumstances) resident in Chapman's London house.

1851   Chapman buys *Westminster Review*; GE becomes assistant editor; meets Herbert Spencer and George Henry Lewes.

1853   Begins to translate Feuerbach's *Das Wesen des Christenthums;* enters intimate relationship with Lewes.

1854   Translation of Feuerbach published as *The Essence of Christianity*; trip to Germany with Lewes (the first of many trips that the couple will make to the Continent over the next twenty years).

1856   Begins to write fiction.

1857   Part I of "Amos Barton" appears in *Blackwood's Edinburgh Magazine,* followed by "Mr. Gilfil's Love-Story" and "Janet's Repentance"; assumes pseudonyn of George Eliot; begins work on *Adam Bede.*

1858   *Scenes of Clerical Life* published, 2 vols. (William Blackwood and Sons, Edinburgh, publishers of all her novels except *Romola*).

1859   *Adam Bede* published, 3 vols.; at work on *The Mill on the Floss.*

1860   *The Mill on the Floss* published, 3 vols.; begins *Silas Marner.*

1861   *Silas Marner* published; works on *Romola,* which begins to appear in serial form in *Cornhill Magazine,* 1862.

1863   *Romola* published, 3 vols. (Smith, Elder & Co.)

1865   Begins work on *Felix Holt, the Radical.*

1866   *Felix Holt* published, 3 vols.

1868   *The Spanish Gypsy* published.

1869   Begins *Middlemarch;* the Leweses become friendly with John Cross (1840–1924).

1871   Publication of *Middlemarch* begins in parts; completed December, 1872.

1874   *The Legend of Jubal and Other Poems* published.

1875   At work on *Daniel Deronda;* decides on parts publication.

1876   February–September, *Daniel Deronda* appears in parts.

1878   At work on *Impressions of Theophrastus Such;* Lewes ill with cancer; Lewes dies November 30.

1880   Marries John Cross, May 6; October, very ill; dies December 22.

Notes on the Editor and Contributors

GEORGE R. CREEGER, Professor of English at Wesleyan University, is the editor and co-editor of several anthologies as well as the author of critical articles on Melville, George Eliot, Salinger, and Capote.

QUENTIN ANDERSON is Professor of English at Columbia University. He is the author of *The American Henry James* (1957).

DAVID R. CARROLL, who is a member of the English Department, Fourah Bay College, Freetown, Sierra Leone, West Africa, has written several articles on George Eliot.

BARBARA HARDY is Professor of English Language and Literature at Royal Holloway College, University of London. In addition to her work on George Eliot she has written *The Appropriate Form: An Essay on the Novel* (1964) and *Charles Dickens: The Later Novels* (1968).

HENRY JAMES (1843–1916), American author. James was one of George Eliot's most perceptive (if also idiosyncratic) early critics.

U. C. KNOEPFLMACHER is Associate Professor of English at the University of California, Berkeley. Besides several articles on George Eliot he has written two books: *Religious Humanism and the Victorian Novel: George Eliot, Walter Pater and Samuel Butler* (1965) and *George Eliot's Early Novels: The Limits of Realism* (1969).

GEORGE LEVINE is Professor of English and Chairman of the Department at Livingston College, Rutgers, The State University. He is the author of *The Boundaries of Fiction: Carlyle, Macauley, Newman* (1968).

DARREL MANSELL, JR. is an Assistant Professor of English at Dartmouth College.

BERNARD J. PARIS, Professor of English at Michigan State University, is the author of *Experiments in Life: George Eliot's Quest for Values* (1965).

THOMAS PINNEY, Associate Professor of English at Pomona College, is the editor of *Essays of George Eliot* (1963).

Selected Bibliography

Primary Texts

Eliot, George. *The Works of George Eliot.* 24 vols. Cabinet Edition. Edinburgh and London: William Blackwood [n.d.]. The standard edition.

Feuerbach, Ludwig. *The Essence of Christianity.* 2nd ed. Trans. George Eliot. Harper Torchbooks. New York: Harper & Row, Publishers, 1957.

Haight, Gordon S., ed. *The George Eliot Letters.* 7 vols. New Haven: Yale University Press, 1954–55.

Pinney, Thomas, ed. *Essays of George Eliot.* London: Routledge and Kegan Paul, 1963.

Anthologies of Criticism

Hardy, Barbara, ed. *"Middlemarch": Critical Approaches to the Novel.* London: University of London, The Athlone Press, 1967.

Haight, Gordon S., ed. *A Century of George Eliot Criticism.* Boston: Houghton Mifflin Company, 1965.

Stang, Richard, ed. *Discussions of George Eliot.* Boston: D. C. Heath & Co., 1960.

Books

Beaty, Jerome. *"Middlemarch" from Notebook to Novel.* Urbana: Illinois University Press, 1960.

Bennett, Joan. *George Eliot: Her Mind and Her Art.* Cambridge: At the University Press, 1948.

Haight, Gordon S. *George Eliot: A Biography.* Oxford: At the Clarendon Press, 1968.

Hardy, Barbara. *The Novels of George Eliot: A Study in Form.* London: University of London, The Athlone Press, 1959.

Harvey, W. J. *The Art of George Eliot.* London: Chatto & Windus, 1961.

Knoepflmacher, U. C. *George Eliot's Early Novels: The Limits of Realism.* Berkeley: University of California Press, 1969.

————. *Religious Humanism and the Victorian Novel: George Eliot, Walter Pater, and Samuel Butler.* Princeton: Princeton University Press, 1965.

Leavis, F. R. *The Great Tradition: George Eliot, Henry James, Joseph Conrad.* New York: New York University Press, 1948.

Noble, Thomas A. *George Eliot's "Scenes of Clerical Life"* (Yale Studies in English, Benjamin Christie Nangle, ed., vol. 159). New Haven: Yale University Press, 1965.

Paris, Bernard J. *Experiments in Life: George Eliot's Quest for Values.* Detroit: Wayne State University Press, 1965.

Speaight, Robert. *George Eliot.* London: Arthur Barker Ltd., 1954.

Stump, Reva. *Movement and Vision in George Eliot's Novels.* Seattle: University of Washington Press, 1959.

Thale, Jerome. *The Novels of George Eliot.* New York: Columbia University Press, 1959.

Willey, Basil. *Nineteenth Century Studies: Coleridge to Matthew Arnold.* London: Chatto & Windus, 1949.

Periodical Articles

Note: The reader should also take account of articles cited in the footnotes (such articles are not listed again here).

Beebe, Maurice. " 'Visions Are Creators': The Unity of *Daniel Deronda,*" *Boston University Studies in English,* I (Autumn, 1955), 166–77.

Carroll, David R. "The Unity of *Daniel Deronda,*" *Essays in Criticism,* IX (October, 1959), 369–80.

Fisch, H. *"Daniel Deronda* or *Gwendolen Harleth?" Nineteenth-Century Fiction,* XIX, No. 4 (March, 1965), 345–56.

Hagan, John. *"Middlemarch*: Narrative Unity in the Story of Dorothea Brooke," *Nineteenth-Century Fiction,* XVI, No. 1 (June, 1961), 17–31.

Harvey, W. J. "George Eliot and the Ominiscient Author Convention," *Nineteenth-Century Fiction,* XIII, No. 2 (September, 1958), 81–108.

Hester, Erwin. "George Eliot's Messengers," *Studies in English Literature,* VII (Autumn, 1967), 679–90.

Knoepflmacher, U. C. "The Post-Romantic Imagination: *Adam Bede,* Wordsworth and Milton," *ELH,* XXXIV (December, 1967), 518–40.

Leavis, F. R. "George Eliot's Zionist Novel," *Commentary,* XXX (October, 1960), 317–25.

Luecke, Sr. Jane Marie. "Ladislaw and the *Middlemarch* Vision," *Nineteenth-Century Fiction,* XIX, No. 1 (June, 1964), 55–64.

Lyons, Richard S. "The Method of *Middlemarch,*" *Nineteenth-Century Fiction,* XXI, No. 1 (June, 1966), 35–47.

Mansell, Darrel, Jr. "George Eliot's Conception of Tragedy," *Nineteenth-Century Fiction,* XXII, No. 2 (September, 1967), 155–71.

Paris, Bernard J. "Toward a Revaluation of George Eliot's *The Mill on the Floss,*" *Nineteenth-Century Fiction,* XI, No. 1 (June, 1956), 18–31.

Poston, Lawrence, "Setting and Theme in *Romola,*" *Nineteenth-Century Fiction,* XX, No. 4 (March, 1966), 355–66.

Preyer, Robert. "Beyond the Liberal Imagination: Vision and Unreality in *Daniel Deronda,*" *Victorian Studies,* IV, No. 1 (September, 1960), 33–54.

Robinson, Carole. "*Romola:* A Reading of the Novel," *Victorian Studies,* VI, No. 1 (September, 1962), 29–42.

————. "The Severe Angel: A Study of *Daniel Deronda,*" *ELH,* XXXI (September, 1964), 278–300.

Thomson, Fred C. "*Felix Holt* as Classic Tragedy," *Nineteenth-Century Fiction,* XVI, No. 1 (June, 1961), 47–58.

————. "The Theme of Alienation in *Silas Marner,*" *Nineteenth-Century Fiction,* XX, No. 1 (June, 1965), 69–84.

Welsh, Alexander, "George Eliot and the Romance," *Nineteenth-Century Fiction,* XIV, No. 3 (December, 1959), 241–54.

TWENTIETH CENTURY VIEWS

British Authors

JANE AUSTEN, edited by Ian Watt (S-TC-26)
THE BEOWULF POET, edited by Donald K. Fry (S-TC-82)
BLAKE, edited by Northrop Frye (S-TC-58)
BYRON, edited by Paul West (S-TC-31)
COLERIDGE, edited by Kathleen Coburn (S-TC-70)
CONRAD, edited by Marvin Mudrick S-TC-53)
DICKENS, edited by Martin Price (S-TC-72)
JOHN DONNE, edited by Helen Gardner (S-TC-19)
DRYDEN, edited by Bernard N. Schilling (S-TC-32)
T. S. ELIOT, edited by Hugh Kenner (S-TC-2)
FIELDING, edited by Ronald Paulson (S-TC-9)
FORSTER, edited by Malcolm Bradbury (S-TC-59)
HARDY, edited by Albert Guérard (S-TC-25)
HOPKINS, edited by Geoffrey H. Hartman (S-TC-57)
A. E. HOUSMAN, edited by Christopher Ricks (S-TC-83)
SAMUEL JOHNSON, edited by Donald J. Greene (S-TC-48)
BEN JONSON, edited by Jonas A. Barish (S-TC-22)
KEATS, edited by Walter Jackson Bate (S-TC-43)
D. H. LAWRENCE, edited by Mark Spilka (S-TC-24)
MARLOWE, edited by Clifford Leech (S-TC-44)
ANDREW MARVELL, edited by George deF. Lord (S-TC-81)
MILTON, edited by Louis L. Martz (S-TC-60)
MODERN BRITISH DRAMATISTS, edited by John Russell Brown (S-TC-74)
OSCAR WILDE, edited by Richard Ellmann (S-TC-87)
RESTORATION DRAMATISTS, edited by Earl Miner (S-TC-64)
SAMUEL RICHARDSON, edited by John Carroll (S-TC-85)
SHAKESPEARE: THE COMEDIES, edited by Kenneth Muir (S-TC-47)
SHAKESPEARE: THE HISTORIES, edited by Eugene M. Waith (S-TC-45)
SHAKESPEARE: THE TRAGEDIES, edited by Alfred Harbage (S-TC-40)
G. B. SHAW, edited by R. J. Kaufmann (S-TC-50)
SHELLEY, edited by George M. Ridenour (S-TC-49)
SPENSER, edited by Harry Berger, Jr. (S-TC-80)
LAURENCE STERNE, edited by John Traugott (S-TC-77)
SWIFT, edited by Ernest Tuveson (S-TC-35)
THACKERAY, edited by Alexander Welsh (S-TC-75)
DYLAN THOMAS, edited by Charles B. Cox (S-TC-56)
YEATS, edited by John Unterecker (S-TC-23)